BUT NEVER
EAT OUT
ON A
SATURDAY
NIGHT

BUT NEVER EAT OUT ON A SATURDAY NIGHT

An Appetizing Glimpse Behind the Scenes in All Kinds of Great American Restaurants

Jim Quinn

DOLPHIN BOOKS
Doubleday & Company, Inc.
Garden City, New York
1983

Copyright acknowledgments for BUT NEVER EAT OUT ON A SATURDAY NIGHT by James Quinn.

Several chapters were previously published in the following publications:

"Hail to the Chef," copyright © 1979 by Municipal Publications, Inc. First appeared in *Philadelphia Magazine*, July 1979.

"Diner," copyright © 1978 by Municipal Publications, Inc. First appeared in *Philadelphia Magazine*, June 1978.

"Mad As a Batter," copyright © 1981 by NJM Associates. First appeared in *New Jersey Monthly*, July 1981.

"Smiles of the Summer Night," copyright © 1982 by the Philadelphia *Inquirer*.

"But Never Eat Out on a Saturday Night" originally published as "Rules to Eat By," copyright © 1983 by the Philadelphia *Inquirer*.

"Why It Tastes So Bad" originally published as "Make Mine Moink," copyright © 1982 by Minneapolis *Star* and *Tribune*. First appeared in *Harper's*, August 1982.

Library of Congress Cataloging in Publication Data
Quinn, Jim.
But never eat out on a Saturday night.

1. Restaurants, lunch rooms, etc.—United States.
I. Title.
TX909.Q56   1983   647'.973
ISBN: 0-385-18220-1
Library of Congress Catalog Card Number 82–45449

Copyright © 1983 by Jim Quinn

ALL RIGHTS RESERVED
PRINTED IN THE UNITED STATES OF AMERICA
FIRST EDITION

*For Rotem,
sentimental favorite and
severest inspiration.*

CONTENTS

Preface	*ix*
PROLOGUE BUT NEVER EAT OUT ON A SATURDAY NIGHT	*1*
ONE HAIL TO THE CHEF	*5*
TWO DINER	*41*
THREE MARIO MAKES THE DOUGH	*71*
FOUR MAD AS A BATTER	*89*
FIVE BEHIND THE CHOW MEIN CURTAIN	*109*
SIX WHY McDONALD'S SUCCEEDED SO WELL	*123*
SEVEN AN ALTERNATIVE EDEN	*131*
EIGHT SMILES OF A SUMMER NIGHT	*143*
NINE WHY IT TASTES SO BAD	*155*
TEN TEST YOUR OWN	*167*

PREFACE

Fifteen years ago, when Lyndon Johnson was still fooling many of the people much of the time about the war in Vietnam and I first started reviewing restaurants, eating out was a celebration of the great occasions of life—things like graduations, engagements, fellowships, anniversaries and divorces. Decor leaned heavily on false marble pilasters and swaths of drapes. Service seemed modeled on a Hollywood director's idea of the last hours of the *Titanic*—when aged retainers went on with their usual duties, loyal, mournful, prescient and inept. The food was modeled on the last days of *haute* (and *faux*) *cuisine:* flounder called *sole* with almonds called *almondine* or *meunière;* steak with adjectives; duck *à* or *au* or *al* or *alla* or *olla orange;* mushy puddings called *pot de crème* or *flan*.

Things were bad. But things got better.

Restaurants are part of all our lives now. A meal is not a celebration—it's a form of entertainment. Cheaper than a play, more satisfying than a movie, more enjoyable than a party, restaurants have gone from being imitation palaces to surrogate family dining rooms. The service is younger, more cheerful, more expert at getting the food to the table while it's still hot enough to eat—and no longer exclusively male. The menus have less bad spelling and more real food.

This book is about the new American restaurants—from expensive *haute cuisine* palaces to fast food shops. About how they work and how they all manage to succeed in their very different ways. Writing this, wandering at will through a series of restaurant kitchens, I found the answer to lots of questions I never knew enough to ask: How does a good waiter remember who gets what dish? Why are some chopsticks in Chinese restaurants so warped they seem bowlegged? Why is pizza crust sometimes crunchier in cold weather? How come french fries don't taste like potatoes? And how much does a dishwasher pay for a pair of shoes?

I also met a lot of restaurant people—the independent, aggressive and skilled workers who make restaurants succeed. Again and again they told me that they'd tried office work—but that sitting still, passing papers, working typewriters or word processors "made me crazy." I think this is because America is being robbed of work. At least, work is now something that machines do—while people watch and tend them. Except in the restaurant industry, where everything is labor intensive and where the quality of the restaurant depends not only on the amount but also on the quality of the work. So restaurants have become a kind of refuge for the skilled worker, the kind of person who needs to feel he or she has done the job well—and needs to feel paid well for doing it.

You may not find all that. But if you've ever wondered what it would be like to start a restaurant—this is what you'd be in for. And once you've seen what it's like behind the door to the kitchen, you'll never be able to go into a restaurant again without noticing some detail in the service or the food—even in the way the butter is served—that tells you all about all the thought, and sweat, and work, that has gone into your seemingly effortless meal.

BUT NEVER
EAT OUT
ON A
SATURDAY
NIGHT

PROLOGUE

BUT NEVER EAT OUT ON A SATURDAY NIGHT

It's almost impossible to be certain of getting good food every time you go to a restaurant—the world just isn't made that way. But it's easy to make sure you're not getting the worst possible food.

For example, no matter how good the restaurant is, never eat out on a Saturday night. That's when intimate, romantic restaurants turn loud and raucous, when big, cheerful, bustling restaurants turn distraught and frantic, when you'll be one hundredth instead of one tenth or one twentieth of your waiter's earnings (so he won't have the time, even if he has the inclination, to give you good service). And most important of all, Saturday nights are so rushed and hectic that many restaurants with famous chefs hire part-time underchefs to help out with the extra work—underchefs who are not nearly as famous, usually for very good reasons.

So never eat out on a Saturday night; any other day is bound to be better. Except for Mother's Day, of course—never, *never* eat out on Mother's Day.

There are, of course, exceptions to every rule, but to be on the safe side:

Never eat in an empty restaurant. Everybody who's not there must know something.

Never eat in a suburban restaurant where there's a square yard of Masonite laid over the indoor-outdoor carpeting to serve as a dance floor and where there's a man in a toupee playing double bass with his hands and a sock cymbal with his left foot, and another man playing an electric organ that sounds like a thousand kazoos almost in tune, with yet another man switching back and forth between violin and sax, and the female vocalist coming on after they play "Satin Doll" to sing "The Boy from Ipanema."

Never eat in a downtown hotel, no matter what the town.

Never order veal if it costs no more than chicken.

Never eat in a place that offers you all the beer or root beer you can drink if you'll pay $9.95 for a ten-ounce steak that looks like a charcoal log and tastes like a burned matchstick. And if you do eat in one of these places, stay out of the men's room, where all the thirsty little boys and thirsty big fathers go to sigh away their greed.

Never order a martini in a Chinatown restaurant.

Never order a drink by brand unless you sit at the bar and watch the bartender make it.

Never eat in a restaurant where the waiters dress like pirates or jockeys or cowboys or apache dancers—or anything but waiters.

Never order fried shellfish the first time you go to any restaurant.

Never eat in places with tables as long as a football field and as wide as your elbow, where you sit in a row with dozens of other people and have to turn sideways in your chair to see the show.

Never eat in a restaurant that calls itself a nightclub.

Never eat in a gambling casino.

Never eat in a restaurant with a souvenir shop attached.

Never eat in any place that makes money off anything but food and drink.

PROLOGUE

Never eat in the French restaurant in a college town.

Never eat in any restaurant recommended by anybody who teaches in a college, goes to a college or is remotely connected to a college—unless it's Chinese.

Never order chop suey or chow mein.

Never order pancakes in an all-night restaurant—unless you like them tasting like hamburgers.

Never eat in a restaurant where the waitresses—or even worse, the waiters—wear their shirts open so you can see their belly buttons.

Never eat in a restaurant the week after it gets a good review.

Never order the catch of the day if it's flounder or sole—it's likely to be the catch of every day, waiting in the freezer and thawed to order.

Never eat in a restaurant where the menu is larger than the table, the pepper mill larger than your date and the baked potato larger than your steak.

Never eat in a place where the menu is covered with an illiterate imitation of Middle English spelling—even if the food *is* good, you'll ruin your digestion laughing over things like Chyken Breaft, Caefar Falad and Fuckling Pig.

Never order a steak that costs less than $10.

Never order surf and turf.

Never order a Caesar salad unless it's made at your table.

Never order the cheapest thing on the menu—except kidneys in a very good French restaurant.

Never order a carafe of wine without checking the wine list to see whether there isn't a bottle of wine at nearly the same price. Never pay more for a single carafe of Gallo Hearty Burgundy than the liquor store charges for four liters of the stuff.

Never eat in a date bar.

Never order a drink that comes with a paper umbrella.

Never order coffee if it comes in a plastic disposable cup.

Never eat in an airplane.

Never, never, *never* eat in an airport.

Never eat in a restaurant that has portraits of Our Past Presidents on the wall, brass American eagles over the door, an American flag anywhere in evidence or patriotic slogans on the placemats. Dr. Johnson said that patriotism was the last refuge of scoundrels—now it's the first refuge of restaurant owners who are losing business (usually for very good reasons).

ONE

HAIL TO THE CHEF

It is not a mere figment of speech, it is a mere statement of fact to say that a French cook will spit in the soup—that is, if he is not going to drink it himself . . . And the waiter dips his fingers in the gravy—nasty, greasy fingers which he is forever running through his brilliantined hair. A customer orders, for example, a piece of toast. Somebody, pressed with work in a cellar deep underground, has to prepare it. All he knows is that it must look right and must be ready in three minutes. Some large drops of sweat fall from his forehead to the toast. Why should he worry? Presently the toast falls among the filthy sawdust on the floor. Why trouble to make another piece? It is much quicker to wipe the sawdust off. Roughly speaking, the more one pays for food, the more sweat and spittle one is obliged to eat with it.

GEORGE ORWELL
Down and Out in Paris and London, 1933

[Otto's] right knee is callused from kneeling before the stove. He has an Oxbridge accent and a Debrettian flourish of names—not one of which he will allow me to divulge. He would like to see his work described. But in this time, in this country, his position is awkward, for he prefers being a person to becoming a personality; his wish to be acknowledged is exceeded by his wish not to be celebrated, and he could savor recognition only if he could have it without publicity . . . Picking up a knife now, he extends his fingers beyond the handle to pinch the blade. He rocks his wrist, and condenses a pile of parsley. There are calluses on his fingers where they pinch the blade.

JOHN MCPHEE
The New Yorker,
February 1979

Two quotes from very similar writers, reflecting their very dissimilar times.

George Orwell takes his British socialist conscience into the kitchens of the most expensive restaurants in Paris in the middle of the Great Depression—and finds suffering and exploitation, and a little unappetizing worker sabotage to frighten the rich with.

John McPhee is romantic and American, and his contemporary ecological conscience leads him to discover Otto, a chef who works alone in a tiny country restaurant he owns, a chef who does nothing by halves or by shortcut or compromise, a chef who will not even allow his real name to be used in the article. People might discover his restaurant: crowds mean success, success means ruin. Small is beautiful; and to Otto, the monk of St. Gastronome, tiny is salvation.

Like all writers, Orwell and McPhee found exactly what they wanted to find. Like all writers with a conscience, they set out to convince us that what they found is exactly what anybody would find. And like all good writers, they succeed superbly—because they're so naively dishonest.

Selectivity has its place in both propaganda and journalism —you just eliminate a couple of facts and everything is easier to summarize. And there is nothing like damning (or canonizing) your subject matter to make your writing seem important. French kitchens could not have been as bad as Orwell says. And Otto, at least according to Mimi Sheraton, the New York *Times* food critic who found out who he was and visited his tiny rural Pennsylvania restaurant, was not nearly as good as McPhee said.

Life, which is merely stranger than fiction, is always more complicated than journalism.

But that fact has not stopped the chef from becoming the superstar of the eighties—something between a rock star and a leader of a back-to-nature movement. Charity groups which used to have fund-raising dances now have demonstration lunches, where you not only eat the food—you learn how to make it—like Holy Communions with directions for transubstantiating on your own. Chefs appear on television giving recipes—or hints, or tips. Successful restaurants spawn successful cooking schools. Add in the new exercise craze and you have a picture of the new America: a nation that jogs on its stomach.

But all the concentration seems to be on the flash and hobby aspect of restaurants—chefs who started out as lawyers or housewives or social workers, chefs who discovered food from Julia Child or a honeymoon course at Cordon Bleu in Paris. Nothing wrong with that—some of the best restaurants in the country are run by second-career restaurant people.

But a restaurant is first of all a business—not a hobby or an inspired imitation of nineteenth-century cooking techniques.

So I thought I should write about the business of running a restaurant. And the best chef I know for discovering the business at its best is Tell Erhardt, who owns and operates a restaurant in Philadelphia called Tell Erhardt's International Cuisine.

Erhardt is young—not yet forty—and was trained as a chef in Germany under the European apprentice system—he started working in the kitchen at thirteen. He was the big, brisk, German good looks of a television personality—and a ninety-second spot on a TV show syndicated around the country.

Erhardt does demonstrations and demonstration luncheons for charities and shopping-center openings. He operates a cooking school. His restaurant is one of the very best in the Philadelphia area. And best of all, Erhardt is not afraid of publicity —no crowds can swamp his restaurant, no success can ruin it. Things are too well organized for that.

Spending a couple weeks in the kitchen with Erhardt and his staff convinced me that Orwell was right about one thing—a lot of very hard work goes into making good food. My legs started giving out after eight hours or so of standing—no more than two thirds through the long restaurant day.

But restaurant workers also get big rewards. Salaries are high ($30,000 to $40,000 a year for a *sous-chef*) and there are fringe benefits: a staff lunch that is really a dinner, a drink or two at the end of the night. Like any small businessman who employs professionals, Erhardt makes sure to treat his people well.

And McPhee is right—at least about the ecology of a good restaurant. At Erhardt's not a scrap of food is wasted, and everything is fresh. Or almost everything.

"Not shrimp and not Dover sole," says Erhardt. "You have to get them frozen. People tell me they have fresh Dover sole in this country and I tell them the only way you can have that is if they swim over. Because if you import them, the law is they have to be frozen. But you have to defrost them right— you get them whole, you leave them in the refrigerator to thaw two days. Then you skin them and prepare them for the waiter to bone. Dover sole—they should have laws in this country about what they call 'Dover sole.' Lots of places it is only flounder. You can tell the difference from the fillet. Dover sole has to be long narrow fillets because that's how the bones run. Flounder is wide fillets. You tell people to look next time they order sole and they can tell."

We are riding, at five-thirty in the morning, through a grimy soaking dawn to the Food Distribution Center of Philadelphia, where Erhardt does all his fish and vegetable shopping. The center, a big truck lot full of boxlike buildings and loading docks, sprawls in a deserted section of the city near its airport.

Tell's truck grinds and strains under the pressure of his driving —"I only have two speeds," he says. "Stop—and fast." His manager, Joe Clement, sits in the back, jolted now and then by the bigger potholes on the empty crumbling roads. Erhardt has a slight but noticeable German accent and what he calls a "German" sense of humor. He drives like someone who likes driving and talks like someone who likes talking.

"The restaurant is a business," he says. "It has to be. And the customer is right, I don't care what he says. One time when I just open, a customer asks for some salt butter. I say to the waiter you go back and tell them that as long as I own this restaurant I only serve sweet butter. Salt butter is for the supermarkets so it doesn't go bad on the shelf. So it turns out this customer is a restaurant reviewer and I get a lousy review. Which says the food 'has no love in it.' This is the first time I ever heard salt butter is called 'love.' So now if you ask for salt butter, I send somebody out to the supermarket and get you some. But I still don't keep it in my restaurant.

"Oleo I do keep. You are going to see this so I will tell you now. For the roux for cream soups we use oleo. First, it is lighter. You go to a restaurant and you can't digest for hours and hours after, it is because of too much butter and cream. I use butter and cream—I like it—sweet butter only and only whipping cream. But in the roux—you can't taste it. I beat in butter flurries to top off the soup, then I add cream . . . It is a beautiful soup. And not so expensive. You see, Joe, already I tell all the secrets. After this article a hundred readers open up a restaurant. They find out how easy it is."

Tell and Joe go over the facts and figures of the restaurant as we drive. The seating capacity is one hundred; on the five days the restaurant is open, it serves six hundred to seven hundred meals. The gross for 1977 was about $500,000; for 1978, $600,000; for 1979, $750,000. There are twenty-eight people working in the restaurant: eight people to wait table, four dishwashers, two chefs who serve as Tell's assistants, a pastry chef, two cooks (who run the cold side of the kitchen—the salad and appetizer courses—and who help out on the hot side on busy nights), two cold-side apprentices, a manager, a maître d', a hostess, a general secretary, a secretary to deal with all the mail from the TV shows, a cleaning woman and three bartenders.

"And a little jazz group that came in right after I am open and asked to play. You will see, they are great. I pay the people good. It is important that they get paid well. Only one person, Georges Perrier [who owns Philadelphia's Le Bec Fin] pays more than me. And he has only one chef, not three. So they know even if they want to leave, they can't make as much. But even more, you will see that you have to involve people. I learn this working at my other American jobs. You know I am first here in America working for the Marriott. I am down the Labor Relations Board ten times in the first six months. Not because I am doing anything wrong. I never lose a case. But I am German—in Germany they do things different. When I learn in my apprenticeship, I was allowed to make any mistake —once. Then the second time they kick where you don't like it. Not the best kind of motivation. But a very effective kind. In America you have to involve the workers in order to motivate them. So when we make up the menu, my chefs are helping. We make lots of decisions together. Once in while, of course, I have to say, 'This is my restaurant, and one, two, three, we do it this way.' But I don't like if the recipe is not popular that they just say, well you wanted it that way. We try out a couple fish recipes at lunch maybe, see which one the waiters say the customer likes. Then we do that for dinner. Everybody has to know they are important. And needed. And that if it is necessary, I can do their job for six days until we get a replacement."

Erhardt began shopping at the Food Distribution Center two years after he opened his restaurant in 1977. Before that he had been buying from restaurant food purveyors.

"My accountant calls me in and says, 'Listen, Tell, your costs are too high, you are losing money.' So I have to figure out what to do. I can't cut back on food. So I shop for myself. It makes my old suppliers angry because they lose a pretty good business—I spend thirty-five hundred dollars a week on food in 1979—but from them I always get one price. Tomatoes always so much a case, limes so much. Last week, the first of the season's crop comes in and the price at the Food Distribution Center drops by half. Before, I didn't know really what was going on. I have to depend on the suppliers to let me know what's in season. Now I see myself. I see what's good. I pick up what's good and load it on the truck. It is hard work, getting up at three or four in the morning, and I will probably leave early tonight—maybe nine o'clock instead of midnight. It makes a long day. But if you are going to do it, you have to do it right.

"A restaurant can buy from food purveyors and make money. They say to me they are averaging costs—sometimes they make more off tomatoes, sometimes less. The cost is always the same, which is making it easier for the accountant. The food you buy is always the same, which is making it easier on the chef. But that is only because you have a lazy accountant who wants the same numbers every week. And a lazy chef who wants to make the same dishes every week. I have a good accountant. I have good people with creativity working for me. And I am the chef."

DOING IT RIGHT—THE MONEY

Erhardt figures his food costs at about 35 percent, his salaries and overhead at 57 percent. Plus a few extras.

"I have to have fresh flowers. There is a waitress, Christl Eggstein, she is married to Johann, the maître d'. She also does the flower arrangements. Then I have to have a doily under the soup plates and coffee cups. It just looks right to me to have it. It must be there.

"Then we have losses. My wife, she drinks tea and we have to have tea made with boiling water in my restaurant. If she sees a cup of tea with šcum on the top, she knows the water is not boiled and everybody is in trouble. And we can't use tea bags because—she is right—that tea is not good enough. So we use tea balls. And people steal the tea balls. Just for a souvenir, maybe. But it adds up. Now I am switching to strainers that fit on the cup. Very pretty stainless steel or chrome strainers. And harder to steal. We have lemon with tea and we have a little chrome squeezer so you don't have to make your fingers messy. So people steal the squeezers instead of the strainers. I can't do anything about that except if the waiter sees the strainer is missing, he puts it on the bill. One lemon squeezer, a dollar and a half. Then suddenly the customer finds the lemon squeezer on the ground or something. Silver I lose also. Also I have a vase of flowers in the ladies room. Sometimes they take a flower. It costs me money but I laugh about it. But sometimes—they steal the vase."

We walk among the fruits and vegetables in a big half-open cinder-block building—something like a line of garages with a truck-loading platform in front. Sparrows who think the lights are an early dawn fight and flutter in the steel rafters or rise like a cloud of flies from some bit of dropped food.

Tell and Joe talk quietly as they go, figuring what this price means and that price means—whether artichokes are good enough to go on the menu this week or if they should wait till next week when the season is further advanced, the artichokes are better and the prices are lower. They buy a huge tilefish, its head as big as a human face, plus two smaller groupers and a lot of fresh black bass.

"You can't buy grouper after it grows too big," says Joe. "They get full of worms. René—that's our Swiss chef—will love these groupers and the tilefish."

"And the bass," says Tell. "He loves to fish. He gets finished work eleven-thirty or midnight and then gets up and drives around in his Jeep to fish at five A.M. He is my European chef, trained in Switzerland in the European way like me—but more with the Nouvelle Cuisine, with the lighter sauces. René Plattner. My other chef is Ted Gawarzewski. He is from Camden, New Jersey, and he trains at the Culinary Institute here in America. Both are good chefs. Both completely different. René is like full of imagination. Ted is like one, two, three—everything he does exactly right, exactly the same, time after time. I don't know if this is the training—or just the way they are. But I know they are balancing out in the kitchen. You need the steady chefs and you need the imagination too. You see today."

The artichokes are good enough. There is no fresh salmon. Tell and Joe decide at the last minute on a thirty-pound bucket of scallops because they really *are* bay scallops.

"If all the bay scallops in America really came from the bays," says Tell, "you could walk on the water it is so thick with shellfish. Bay scallops in a restaurant can be sea scallops if you're lucky, or the suppliers take a little punch of metal and they punch scallops to size. Out of fluke. Even out of shark. It keeps the shark dangers down anyhow. And if you bread them and fry them you don't know what you're eating in the first place. Could be boiled potato. Tastes like boiled potato, am I right? So never buy breaded scallops—unless you see them breaded."

We wander among the stands looking for raspberries. No raspberries.

"They know me here, because I deal in cash. And because of the TV show. They know Georges Perrier because he has the most expensive restaurant in Philadelphia and he shops here too. They like it, selling to the famous chefs and the fancy restaurants. And they like cash. So I shop for Georges and Georges shops for me. He is down here Fridays. They know if they have good raspberries, I get a case and Georges gets a case. They know if something is good, they put it aside and we take it. If something is bad, they tell me 'This is not your product.' That is what I like to hear—because that's what I am doing here, buying my product."

DOING IT RIGHT—THE CUSTOMER

"The customer has to be right. If I don't do it for him, somebody else will. So you call my restaurant. First of all the phone is answered after two rings. I have an extension in my kitchen. I hear the phone ring three times in my restaurant, I blow my top. What is everybody, asleep? Then we take the time, we say,

'Hello, this is Tell Erhardt's International Cuisine, can I help you?' In a pleasant voice, no matter what is going on or how you are feeling today. When you make a reservation, somebody checks the book to write it down, takes your number so we can call you back the day of the reservation to make sure you are coming. And there are a few people, a little list in the beginning of the book, who are not welcome in the restaurant. Not many. Somebody who comes five or six times and is always getting drunk and abusive. One woman. Only one thing worse than a drunk woman is two drunk women. This woman throws up all through the meal. On purpose she goes in the ladies room and sticks her finger down her throat after every course and then at the end orders a lot of ice cream scoops and three desserts and then goes and throws up again. We can't have this. It is too . . . decadent, you know? And it messes up the ladies room.

"When you come in the restaurant, you are greeted nicely by the hostess. You do not stand around for your table. I hate this. Just like I hate when restaurants ask you to leave your table. We seat one hundred. We do not book more than one hundred eighty, one hundred eighty-five for our two seatings. After this number the service starts to break down. Saturday nights we have only two seatings still. Not true of many restaurants. One seating is at six and when you make the reservation we tell you that the second is at nine o'clock. During the week if you come in and your table is not ready, I come out of the kitchen and go to the customers and say, 'Look, it takes the same time if you get angry or not. Please let me buy you a round of drinks and your table is ready by the time you are finished.'

"We never ask people to leave. Never. What am I going to do? Some guy talks to his girl so he can get laid and I tell him he takes too long? He doesn't score. I lose a customer. Even the girl nine times out of ten is unhappy, right? So you just have to let him alone. Good food takes time. Enjoying good food takes time.

"The maître d' takes the order. He oversees the service. All my service is European. That means the waiters bring out the food in copper serving pans, put a serving cart next to the table, serve from that. My waiters and waitresses—European service does not mean only men do it, though some American restaurants think they cannot have women. I always have women.

"Then the waiter brings the wine list, because we want to sell you wine. I used to sell two bottles a table. Especially to people who know wine, because they also know bargains. Now I charge more, sell less, don't have problems running out—and make less money. My list is still one of the best in the city and I still have bargains for my customers. Years ago I got this buy on Château d'Yquem '62, a great year and a great wine that is wonderful with dessert. I got it for one hundred twenty-eight dollars a case. This same wine at the Palace in New York is six hundred dollars a bottle. Retail, a couple of hundred if you could ever find it. So I have a bottle on ice, open, on my dessert cart—you can have a glass of this wine for four dollars. A beautiful wine. One that most people would never get to taste. Except here. And what is four dollars? You tell your friends. Your friends become my customers too.

"All right. You order, the waiter brings in the order to the kitchen. Then, and only then, the food is cut. You order veal, we cut the veal off the side of the veal. You order pork, we slice the pork. This is important. You go home tonight in your own kitchen. You take a piece of meat and cut one slice off. Leave the slice a couple hours. You can see it darken up. Some restaurants slice once a day. Some once a week. Some buy sliced-up portions and keep them in the freezer. This is all changing the meat color and the taste and the texture. We can't have this. We slice to order.

"But we don't cook yet. The meat goes on a tray next to my stove—my stove is fourteen hundred degrees on the top—you will see what that means when you stand near it and sweat. We put the meat beside. The waiter comes in and says, 'Pickup.'

"Then he knows in two minutes he has to be back and pick up the food. With my heat I cook everything in less time. But I have no heat lamps for the food to stay hot under. Because it dries it out. No steam table for vegetables. We part-cook vegetables and then finish them to order in the serving pan. We do have a heat lamp—we put bread under it, after it goes into the oven to crisp the crust. And every twenty minutes or so we have fresh bread from the oven. We have a steam table—for sauces. The waiter must pick up in time; he must know it is going to be ready in time. No standing in front of the chair waiting while the customer is waiting too—in an empty dining room. The waiter clears your appetizer or he sees you are finished your drink, he gives you a second to breathe, and then into the kitchen and 'Pickup.'

"Now you are served—European service. Entrees in a copper pan. Vegetables in another copper pan. If you order a large entree—duck is very big—it doesn't look good on the plate. So we cut the duck in half; we keep the other half warm on the serving cart. Then when you are finished one half, the waiter brings a clean plate, some more vegetables, and serves the second half. This way it looks right.

"You finish your entree. The waiter crumbs the table. He runs over it with this little . . . machine so it is clean. He takes off the salt and pepper. Any waiter who serves dessert with salt and pepper still on the table, it costs him five dollars—we put it in a box and save it to spend on the Christmas party. But we don't have too much five dollars. Then the waiter puts down a spoon and fork on the table and serves coffee.

"Any staff passing sees a fork and spoon and knows that this table should see the dessert cart. Nobody needs to tell anybody anything. You don't need to have all these conversations of waiters. You just have to have things right. No busboys in my restaurant. Anybody who comes back to the kitchen brings something. No 'one waiter for one customer.' We pool all the tips. We staple the tip to the bill so we can see if the customer didn't leave so much—maybe he is unhappy and we try to find out why. We divide the tips among the waiters and headwaiters on a point system based on seniority. This way, nobody is passing a table and saying, 'That's not my job.' Everybody is interested in making the customer as happy as possible. If you are unhappy, I try to find out. I walk through the dining room two or three times in the night, ask everybody how is everything, did you enjoy yourself. If we do something wrong, I apologize—we have to make the second effort.

"Last Saturday I have a fight with my hostess, now I have to get a new one. I told her apologize to this table, give them a bottle of champagne, tell them desserts are on the house. The hostess says she did not even see what happened and why should she apologize. *But we dropped water! We dropped water on the table!* We can't have this. We can't have arguing about it either. The customer goes home and never comes back!

"I have signs in my kitchen all about customers and how you only keep them if you are not careless with them, that the customer is not an interruption in my job—he *is* my job—and lots of sayings. Sometimes everybody laughs at my famous signs for being corny. But the customer is right—and we are all supposed to know it."

NINE A.M.—"I NEED A MINUTE"

"I need a minute quiet," says Erhardt, sitting at the butcher-block table that fills one corner of the large kitchen. "You be surprised, Cindy, if you sit down and have a cup of coffee, the parsley is still there afterward."

Cindy Perlstein laughs and switches off the Cuisinart. She has been separating the new parsley from the Food Distribution Center into sprigs that are good enough for decoration, stems that will go into a stock or soup, and sprigs that are minced in the machine. Cindy is a graduate of the Culinary Institute and runs the cold side weekdays; weekends the cold side is taken over by Vicki Weiss and Cindy moves to the hot side to work with the chefs.

The only other person in the kitchen is Tippi Meesiri, the twenty-one-year-old pastry chef, who was born in Thailand and who learned to cook by working in her family's restaurant and pastry shop. She has been separating the strawberries—

fancy ones for garnish, unripe ones to put in the refrigerator, fully ripe or soft ones to mix with any leftovers from last week and a little Grand Marnier to make into a strawberry sorbet.

Cindy brings coffee. Tippi brings Tell a plate of grapefruit from which all the skin and white fiber has been carefully trimmed.

"I am on the Scarsdale diet," says Tell. "Two days, eight pounds. But it is hard to diet when I'm working—I get too weak. But this is the way to do the Scarsdale diet, huh? Today I need to have grapefruit for breakfast and poached chicken for lunch. Tippi makes the grapefruit for me. And I make poached chicken for lunch—for the whole restaurant."

THE BACK ROOM IS THE FRONT DOOR

Erhardt's restaurant takes up the first floor of the Chestnut Hill Hotel—a big old country building with a three-story portico and huge columns. If you look around the parking lot at the back, you can see the small patches of mint and basil and parsley and chives that grow there in the summer months. A few more herbs grow in a side window box. The part of the restaurant that a customer sees—the front—is a big dining room with white walls, fresh flowers and lots of paintings that Erhardt rotates from week to week because he can't help fussing with them.

"I want a little more color in this corner," he says, and everything is hung again. Near the reservations desk is what Tell calls the "Sweat Wall"—a display of plaques and awards and memberships in various professional or food societies like the Chaine des Rôtisseurs and the Companions of Barsac and Sauternes.

Across the small foyer is the bar and a smaller dining room called Cafe Tell.

"I keep it dark in here," he says. "My main dining room is light. I like the people to see the food. To read the menu without holding it over the candle. Some people—maybe they have reasons not to want bright lights—they can eat in Cafe Tell. It is a nice room. One guy we see every three months and he comes three times in one week, first with a bunch of university professors. Then two nights later with two women in their forties or fifties. Then two nights later with three women—in their twenties. Always he eats in Cafe Tell. And each night he make the reservation in a different name. And we have to be sure to call him by that name. We never never ask why, but he tells us anyway. Business reasons. And I believe him. But he must have *some* business, right?"

Behind the bar is a piano, wedged in one corner, and it is here that the trio sets up on Saturday night. The bar does not do a very big business, says Tell, but that is probably because he counts on it as a holding area for his reservations.

Behind the main dining room is another large room—maybe twenty feet by twenty feet, that holds the dishwasher, all the rows of glassware, the refrigerator for white wines and champagne, the ice machine and a small coffee machine that can only make eight cups at a time.

"My waiters hate this coffee machine," says Erhardt. "But this way we always have fresh coffee. Because we use it up so fast."

Behind the dishwashing room is the kitchen—thirty or thirty-five by twenty-five, a huge kitchen for a restaurant this size. Erhardt takes me on a tour and explains as he goes.

"Even if we built on an extra dining room and doubled the size of the restaurant, this kitchen would still be big enough. I don't like crowding together people. I always wanted my own restaurant. I knew what it would be like when I got it."

Three professional stoves take up almost the whole of one long wall. One is mainly used as a staging area, holding pans for the parboiled vegetables and the bottles and bowls of oil, clarified butter, heavy cream, salt, pepper and garlic that are used in cooking. The cooking is done on the other two stoves, called "flattops." They have no burners on top at all, only heavy iron plates with sort of rings, like targets, in the center and three-inch holes in the center of the rings. The stoves are already turned on full blast at 9 A.M.; an inch or so of flame pokes up through the center holes. Over the stove is a complicated system of hoods that vent out the cooking smoke and nozzles that automatically foam the whole kitchen in case of fire. The stoves are so hot that if you face them for a minute or so your back feels cool—like standing in front of a fireplace in a cold room. Though it is early September now, and temperatures are still in the high seventies.

Down the middle of the kitchen runs an island with the steam table for sauces, the prep table where the food is cut or chopped to order and the big locker where plates are kept hot enough to keep the food from cooling.

"But not too hot to touch," says Erhardt. "We serve food on plates. We do not cook on them. Nobody has to hand you plates with a napkin wrapped around them, as if they handle melted steel in the foundry. Nobody has to warn you, watch out. Nobody burns their fingers at my tables."

On the side of the island away from the stoves is another long counter—just plain stainless-steel pipes with a six-foot marble top—that is used by Tippi for making pastry early in the day. At dinner hour it becomes the pickup stand for salads and cold appetizers.

Tucked into a corner near the walk-in refrigerator is another table, only four feet long, where all the salads are made. Each station has its own trash can, its own distinct space—and as the kitchen slowly fills up, each person seems to do what has to be done without any direction from anybody else. I've worked in restaurant kitchens myself—very lousy kitchens, for very lousy restaurants, years ago—and the difference in this kitchen is that everybody works constantly; everybody is much younger—Tell at thirty-five is the oldest person in the restaurant; and everybody is sober. The drink of this kitchen is ice water, served in big stainless-steel pitchers and balloon wineglasses.

"We have drinks after, when we clean up," says Tell. "Sometimes in the summer on a Saturday, a beer if the afternoon is ninety degrees. But you can't have too much before you close everything down. It hits you in this heat. Then you're really flying in the kitchen, you don't care what happens. And if you don't care what happens . . . *everything* happens.

"Now, it is ten after nine. I finish my coffee. I make the setup. The hardest hour of the day." He drains his cup, smiles, jumps up, says, "That's why they call me 'chef'!" And begins moving at a half run.

It took me three days of watching this before I could figure out what was happening—even now, I look over my notes and have trouble straightening out just which pans and which pots go on the stove first, just what is done before what. But in two hours, Tell never slows down, hardly ever stops talking—giving me cooking tips, invitations to taste, things to watch for in other restaurants, general advice about life and vegetables, plus an occasional ribald aside.

"You should always wear clogs in the kitchen. I wear them since I start in the kitchen on the first day at thirteen and a half—the half because for six months I was apprentice to a hairdresser until I didn't like it. To keep clogs on, you have to flex your toes, so you don't get legs cramps and the varicose veins . . ."

He fills two twenty-gallon aluminum pots with water, dumps two whole heads of garlic in each and puts them on the stove. They will be the white veal stock and the white chicken stock of the day. He cuts a six-inch onion in half and puts it, cut side down, on the stove to blacken, "so it gives the stock a little color and the flavor is beautiful." He puts ten pounds of butter in another pot to clarify. He fills another twenty-gallon pot with water and adds the peelings of last night's asparagus. The white stems of the asparagus go in another pot with a pound of oleo to cook "until the flavor is out. Then I add flour and cook. It is the roux for my cream of asparagus soup."

Apples, onions and oleo in another pot; after they cook down a little, more flour—the base for mulligatawny soup. "So we can use up all this extra chicken stock from poaching everybody's Scarsdale chicken for lunch. I will add cream and curry—but curry only at the last minute before I add the stock to the roux. Otherwise it turns bitter. You remember when you make curry sauce. Same with paprika."

Each time he moves a pot, he wipes the stove with a towel he keeps tucked under his belt.

"In Germany the stove is called the piano," he says, "and they always say you have to clean the piano. You get in the habit of wiping everything. First of all, this is sensible—you don't know when the Board of Health is walking through. And some of my customers come in through the kitchen, so it has to look nice for them. And—I hate it to be dirty. This is *my* part of the kitchen."

He puts another pot containing hot oil on the stove; when it begins to spit he slides in chopped-up veal bones.

"It costs me a hundred and twenty dollars for a leg of veal. It costs me a hundred and thirty dollars for the whole side of the same veal. Americans don't want this side of veal, because they don't know how to cut it and it is all just waste. But René, my Swiss chef, he cuts it down for me. Along the muscle, takes out all the tough parts, makes the bones small. We make roast so we stew it with dark stock, mushrooms, cream. Put it in a small soufflé dish that holds one cup, top it with hollandaise, run it under the broiler to order so it gets dark and rich looking on the top—it is a beautiful appetizer.

"In this pot I putting bones. Then when they brown, I put carrots and celery and onion and stems of parsley. Then when they brown, I put in some tomato paste. Then I add a little stock or wine, depending on which one I have more of on hand, usually both, and cook it down so it browns again, a beautiful brown coating on the bottom of the pan. Then more wine or stock, stir around to deglaze the bottom. Cook down again. We do this eight times, and then we get a stock. A chef's stock."

In yet another pot, all the huge fish heads and skin, with oil and a little wine "to sweat the fish first—always do this with fish stock, you will taste the difference." Then the pot is filled with water and wine and any fish stock that hasn't been used the night before. "I do not waste this, it has good taste still."

Another pot filled with mushrooms and a little white wine. "You never sauté mushrooms raw. They have too much water and ruin the sauce. I sweat them first in a little oil and white wine and they give off their juices. Then they have a taste you can't get otherwise. The wine I use is Inglenook. Inglenook is the best jug wine, in my opinion. To *cook* with—I never tasted it. But one of the women in my cooking class says she serves it in her house even, so it must be okay to drink. You see how this is cooking down?"

He stirs the browning veal bones, adds wine. Then he puts four big chickens in the twenty-gallon pot of water that is beginning to boil. "If you want to make the stock better, you put the chickens in cold. If you want the *chicken* better, you put the chicken in after the stock comes to a boil. Today we want the chicken to be extra good because the Scarsdale diet says poached chicken for the chef.

"The only way you can tell chicken is done is to pinch the joint—the joint between the drumstick and thigh is best—and if your finger goes to the bone, it is done. Sometimes people in here tell me I undercook chicken because they see the bone is red. I tell them you don't eat the bone. If you want the bone cooked, then you have to have the chicken overcooked—all dried and stringy. Same with pork. Only cook the bone if you are going to eat the bone."

He strains the water from the asparagus peelings. "You only need a little cooking with this because how much can you get from peelings? Now I add the roux. Stir—you taste it." He sticks a finger in the already bubbling soup and nods appreciatively. I stick a finger in and burn the hell out of myself.

"Don't worry—you get used to it in the kitchen. And women like you better if you have warm fingers. Now tonight I add some asparagus to this and it is asparagus soup. Remember, Jim, what many restaurant owners forget—you got to have asparagus in it if you are making asparagus soup."

Another pot and—"Chopped ham, onion and clarified butter, and sauté. Then morels, dark imported dried mushrooms we have already soaked, then a little chopped fresh mushrooms —remember they were sweated in wine and oil first, also a little demiglace—taste this!"

My fingers are not getting used to it—I never do get used to sticking my fingers in boiling stock or butter sauces, which is the way everyone in the kitchen tests everything—but the sauce is extraordinary.

"That's why they call me 'chef'! Demiglace is only veal stock cooked down and thickened with a little flour. The French do not thicken with flour, only cook it days. And days. But you cannot digest food like this—it is too rich. My demiglace is a good demiglace. I tell the ladies in my cooking class you can freeze it in the ice-cube tray. Then when you sauté something, add a little butter to the pan, a cube of demiglace, a little heavy cream or wine—instant sauce!"

He pulls out big plastic tubs from the walk-in refrigerator.

"This one is another veal stock—we make four or five different kinds to keep on hand. This is duck juice. I make my duck so there is no fat in it and the skin is crisp. First, we put them breast down in a pan half-filled with water. In the water, apple cores and peelings that Tippi has left over from the desserts. Onion, carrots, bay leaf, at four hundred fifty-two degrees for one and a half hours—all the fat cooks out from under the breast and the bottom gets brown. Then we pour out the juice, strain it, turn the duck over and roast another hour and a half, breast up, so it browns. Of course, these are big ducks—six or seven pounds. The duck juice we save. We deglaze the pan, we cook the bones, the juice gets all that taste. Part makes a sauce, part goes to cook tomorrow's ducks. I don't like my duck to be all orange juice and green peppercorns or whatever color pepper is the new restaurant fad now. I like my duck to taste *duck*. Then it is"—he slaps his stomach —"food from the chef!"

A twenty-gallon pot of string beans goes on to parboil, along with a pot of spinach for the luncheon quiche.

"You can only use spinach for salad if it is still crisp—if it gets limp like this, I can't serve it. But it still tastes good. It is good for quiche with cheese and custard. You know the quiche in restaurants that gets like scrambled eggs? Because somebody in the kitchen thinks they do the customer a favor and uses too many eggs—you have to use the same volume of cream and of eggs or it will curdle. Here I have some salmon I can't serve as salmon steak, some flounder trimmings, a little butter and mushrooms—it will be another quiche.

"The roux is cooked for the mulligatawny—I take it off the fire because the roux must be lukewarm when you add the boiling stock. If it is hot, you get lumps. If it is cold, you don't get lumps but it takes the sauce or the soup half an hour to heat up, and by that time it burns.

"You get floury soup or sauces? Flour must cook at least twenty minutes—ten in the roux, ten in the sauce. Otherwise you have the raw taste. Here, look—here is the fish stock from yesterday, all natural gelatin—look how it stays! That's what you can't buy! That is a chef's stock!"

In the space of two hours the big stoves have been crowded up with huge aluminum pots and emptied again. All the sauces are in their stainless-steel containers at one end of the steam table, all the soups at the other end. The only way to regulate the heat on the big stoves is by moving the huge pots closer or farther from the flame in the center, so each of the pots has been shifted four or five times—to boil, to simmer, to cook, to cool. Tell's face is flushed from the heat. He stops from time to time to wipe sweat from his face, but otherwise is in constant motion.

"Now I make the *mise en place*—that's what the French call it. You get all the things you need together"—a deep stainless-steel pot full of vegetable oil with a ladle in it, another with clarified butter; a wine bottle filled with wine from the Inglenook jug, another filled with red wine vinegar; a shallow bowl of salt, another of cracked black pepper, another with minced garlic in oil, another with blanched almond slivers, another with minced parsley; and a quart of heavy whipping cream. It is eleven o'clock, half an hour before lunch begins—and Tell is now ready to sit down.

Behind us the kitchen has been filling up. Bob the potman is already at work cleaning the huge pile of pots Tell has built beside his sink. Tippi has fitted the dough into individual ramekins that will hold the luncheon quiches. She runs a line of chopped spinach down the center of half of them, fills the sides with slivers of Gruyère cheese, carefully pours the egg-custard mixture over the cheese and puts the ramekins in the oven to cook. Cindy has torn up new spinach for the spinach salad, made dressing, hard-boiled and then cooled some eggs (they will be hollowed out, then filled with American caviar as an appetizer). The chickens from the big pot have cooled and Cindy is now taking them apart by hand—preserving the breasts whole so they can be cut up for chicken salad. Only the chef will get plain poached chicken—the customers get diced breast mixed with walnuts, pineapple, homemade mayonnaise and unsweetened whipped cream.

René Plattner and Ted Gawarzewski both arrive within minutes of eleven o'clock. Two very different men in their twenties —René is European, drives a Jeep, fishes whenever he can. Medium height, thin, with dark curly hair. He seems to have a love-hate affair with America.

"It is great here. But the food, man, you can't eat it. You can't eat even the mashed potatoes because it is all made from powder or something. You eat these mashed potatoes? It is not even tasting. And how much trouble is it to mash up potatoes? Last week I have a fast-food hamburger. This is the second one since I am in this country and this is the second time I am sick for three days from it. From now on I tell my girl I am eating a raw carrot or something if I don't cook it myself. I don't understand this food. Nothing to eat. Except"—he smiles, delighted with the memory—"except Italian hoagies. Delicious. And if you eat Chinese."

Ted, from Camden, New Jersey, is blond, even thinner than René, drives an American luxury car—and his hobby is disco dancing. I ask him if that isn't a little tiring after a day of standing over a stove.

"Not really. I'm used to it. Sometimes it's a little hard getting up if I don't get too much sleep. Or once in a while I have too many scotches. But I watch that. You come in here once with a hangover, standing over those stoves with the heat blasting at you—you'll never do it again."

"René," says Tell, "even if you have great luck fishing, I got more beautiful fish. Look at this black bass and what shall we do with it?"

A long discussion. This is a delicate fish, says René, but it is one third head, one third bones and only one third flesh. How many reservations tonight? Look at the size of the fish. One fillet is too small. Two fillets is too much for a single portion.

"I make it with port wine sauce? It is delicious," says René. "Even beurre blanc."

Johann Eggstein and his wife, Christl, arrive and begin setting up the dining room. The day bartender arrives. Then two luncheon waiters. Lots of coffee drinking.

"O.K., everybody, you think you could get dressed?" says Tell. "Looks like the Village People in here . . . Today for lunch we have a party of forty who want omelets, so I need a hundred and fifty eggs, Cindy, please. For dinner René is making these beautiful black bass fillets—how about we have some flounder, make it in a mousse, put the flounder on top of the fillet, julienne of vegetables on top, poached in white wine? Sea bass Nouvelle Cuisine!"

René puts the flounder through the big rotary grinder and begins mixing it with whipping cream.

"The French mix the fish mousse with *pâté à chou*—a mixture of flour and egg and potato," says Tell. "It makes the mousse puff up more but it is too floury tasting. I use egg whites beaten over ice. René, you use egg white?"

René demonstrates as he explains: he does not use egg white because it isn't necessary. The fish will puff up fine if it is this fresh. And he doesn't bother with ice cubes because both the flounder and the cream come very cold out of the refrigerator. He simply beats the cream into the ground fish, adds salt and white pepper and a little nutmeg—and he has a light and delicious mousse.

The restaurant is officially open for lunch at eleven-thirty, but nothing seems to be happening in the kitchen yet.

"People have drinks," says Tell. "They sit a minute and look at the menu. We don't get orders till twelve or so. Come outside and see my car."

It is a BMW with a supercharger, a Fuzzbuster and a special

CB radio that is built in so it looks like an ordinary radio. Lots of other extras—a spoiler under the front bumper that came specially from Germany, a racing steering wheel.

"This is a fast car," he says. "At hundred-thirty, hundred-forty you take your hands off the wheel and it just goes along straight. The Germans know how to make cars. And knives. And beer. Chefs too. My CB handle is 'Short Order One.' I'm not kidding. You will see when we do those omelets I am a *fast* chef. I sell this car now and buy the big BMW. I am back with my wife, and she can't drive a stick. So I have a Porsche for myself, and then we sell this and sell her Oldsmobile and get a good car—but with automatic.

"We split up from the restaurant. All these years we plan to have it and then we start to run it together and it is too much. We fight about the restaurant and then we take it home. But my wife always stays a partner and now we are back together and everything is fine because she doesn't work in the restaurant. She does things with the publicity and when I travel she is along. She is part of everything. But we just can't work in the restaurant together.

"Hey, look, the mint comes up! We have mint juleps tonight! You know, I never heard of this drink till two years ago. Joe asks if we can make it for Kentucky Derby. Now I love it! René and me and his girl and Janet, my wife—we all share a house down at the shore—Sunday nights we go down because the place is closed Monday and Tuesday. It is four o'clock in the morning when we get there, we sit on the porch, we make big glasses of mint julep—you have to grow your own mint—half a bottle bourbon in each glass, we watch the sun come up, go for a swim, go to sleep . . . We will have the first mint juleps tonight."

He walks back into the kitchen and touches the mezuzah in the doorway.

"See, help from all sides. We even have a father in to bless the pots. O.K. . . . Ordering . . ."

When the waiter takes an order, he writes it on a pad that makes two copies. Then he comes in the kitchen and writes it out again on the bill. The bill is then stuck in a slotted metal holder so that anyone can find the bill for any table. One copy of the order pad gets stuck on a nail in front of the sauce table; one copy is given to one of the chefs who calls out "Ordering . . ." and reads off the list. Salads are then made to order, meat cut and put on a tray near the stoves. When the waiter needs the food, he simply says, "Table twelve" and everything appears in two minutes.

Even if another waiter has taken the order, he can read what's on the pad—and he knows who gets what because of the "oldest lady."

"The oldest lady in the party is number one," explains Johann. "So what is first on the pad is her order. It goes clockwise around the table from her. Sometimes you cannot tell the oldest lady—then it is the man with the beard—or the striped suit. Or moustache—whatever. You write that on the pad and nobody makes the mistake."

But of course somebody always makes a mistake sooner or later—not at lunch, which goes smoothly and is usually for never more than eighty or a hundred. But on one Saturday night while I was standing in my corner, trying hard to flex my toes and ease the pain in my calves, a waiter came back to the kitchen with terrible news—eight or nine duck halves had gone out of the kitchen in the past ten minutes. Each of them is in a pan cut in two pieces, boned except for the drumstick and one wing joint. But one pan had two breasts.

"Two breasts?" shouts Erhardt. "What does the guy say who got two legs?"

"We can't find him. He must already have eaten it. Maybe he didn't notice it."

"Maybe he didn't notice? Maybe he never comes back! Maybe he writes to the newspaper about famous Tell Erhardt serves four-legged ducks in his restaurant! You got to find him and make the extra effort!"

The customer is never found, so he never gets his bottle of champagne or free dessert—and the letter never appears in the paper. It is possible that the guy just never did notice and was happy with his meal. But it was the disaster of the night for at least five minutes—which is as long as most disasters last.

Then there was the disaster of the customer who wanted the duck completely boned and sautéed in garlic—real minced garlic and not garlic powder.

"This is an insult, you tell him, to think I have anything but real garlic in my restaurant, but we do it. I give him the garlic. Is he Greek? You know—short and dark skin like? Then I give him extra garlic."

The waiter returns, as apologetically as possible—the customer would like some more garlic. We all wait for the explosion.

"I get to like this guy," says Tell. "When we slow down tonight, I go out and visit him. He knows what he likes, anyhow." A dozen cloves of garlic go under the big chopping knife, a little salt—they turn into a powdery snow. A little oil is put in a silver sauceboat; the garlic is mixed into that.

"Jim reads this magazine where the chef has calluses on his fingers from the knife," laughs Tell. "I forgot to tell him what this means. It means the chef doesn't know how to use his knife." Erhardt hands the garlic sauce to the waiter. "Tell the customer it gets stronger if he waits two minutes, and I come to see him at the table. But I stand upwind."

The next crisis is the anniversary cake. A family is taking out Grandpop and Grandmom on their anniversary and wants to bring their own cake. Of course they can—the waiters bring it into the kitchen holding it between them, looking for a silver tray big enough to hold it. The cake is several tiers high and decorated with yellow and blue and pink and green icing.

"Blue cake! Is it made of blueberries? Because if it isn't a blueberry tart, there is *no blue food!* How artificial can you get? Look—the icing falls off the cake—all around. I cannot serve it in my restaurant—what do the other customers think? Tippi, you can do something with this?"

Tippi is already loading a pastry bag with the fallen icing, which has come off in soft two- or three-inch chunks, like sections of a Victorian cornice. She squirts it back in squiggles and swirls that look exactly like the original ones—and that stay on, too. Tell watches, fascinated, like the rest of us.

"This is navy icing. They call it that because they made it in the U.S. Navy. It's true. That's why they lost the war in Vietnam."

The crisis of the forty omelets is not even a crisis at all—it hardly occupies the attention of any of the kitchen staff. Tippi is cleaning out the dessert refrigerator, as she must once a week. Cindy and Ted are cleaning out the big walk-in box—taking out every box of food and tub of stock, tasting, throwing out, washing down floor and walls with grease cutter and germicide. Only three of the five lunch waiters are waiting on the party of forty—the rest serve appetizers and salads from the cold side, or are told they have to wait a few minutes for the hot food—to kind of stall the customers.

"We knock them out one, two, three," says Tell. "What you think I should serve with the omelets? Mushrooms? Zucchini?"

"Zucchini," I say, for no reason.

"O.K. Cindy, please forty green and forty yellow squash in julienne. René sautés them. We have *omelet Quinn* this morning—anybody doesn't like it, you tell them complain to the magazine he writes for and about the Irish taste in food."

Two minutes to chop and one to sauté the squash. The waiters come in and say, matter-of-factly, "Omelet pickup."

Tell has three big black steel frying pans in front of him on the stove, each with a long, highly raised handle. He has his 150 eggs in three separate stainless-steel containers. The first waiter takes nine dishes out of the hot locker and puts them in front of René. Tell loads the three pans with eggs, shakes them sideways, lets them set, gives one a sudden tilt and flip so a lip of the omelet curls up around itself. He moves it to a hotter part of the stove, holds back the set egg with a spatula and tilts the pan so the loose egg runs down and cooks, moves the pan to the hottest part of the stove, gives the second pan a sudden flip and moves it to the second hottest part of the stove, turns the pan of the first omelet over the hot plate René puts in front of him—it is a curled and fluffy omelet—refills the pan with egg, tilts the second pan so the loose egg runs, flips the third so the omelet folds over itself, moves each pan to a new part of the stove, unloads the second omelet—René loads them with the sautéed squash . . .

I can't write it as smoothly and simply as it went. René keeps replacing the plates, the waiters keep replacing the pile, each waiter takes three omelets and disappears. As I watch I am first convinced that there is a kind of assembly-line, rehearsed regularity to the omelet making. But there isn't—sometimes a pan moves to the hottest part a jump ahead of another. Three times Tell turns away from the stove, his face bright red from the heat, and walks to the window, wipes his forehead and exhales suddenly—the way you see batters do in a baseball game when they want to break the tension and concentrate on getting the hit. That takes maybe five or six seconds. The forty omelets are made and gone and Tell looks at the kitchen clock.

"Thirteen minutes and fifty-five seconds! Forty omelets!" He pulls his white pants away from between his legs. "The sweat runs down! I earn my handle, right? 'Short Order One'! *Cooked to order!* What is next, now? Table sixteen pickup—one cheese quiche, one seafood quiche, each split on the plate? Cindy, you make this with some spinach salad or something so it doesn't look ugly, please . . ."

Without a pause, the kitchen goes on with lunch. The high color on Tell's face slowly shades off to the permanent flush from the stoves.

I ask about the system of making omelets.

"System? There is no system. We don't stand around and practice omelets. Everybody knows what they have to do. René, he sees what I am doing and he puts the plates and takes the omelets. The waiters see we need more hot plates and give them to us. You can't have a system on the stove because the pans get hot different ways. And even mixed, the eggs cook different —I am a chef, not like some high school kid making Egg McMuffin two minutes on a side with a timer. I cook the omelets till they turn into omelets. How long is that—forty omelets, thirteen minutes fifty-five seconds? Thirty-five seconds an omelet?"

The way I figure it, it is just under twenty-one seconds an omelet. I never get a chance to say that because Tell interrupts me.

"A ketchup bottle?"

"The customer wants ketchup on the omelet," says the waiter.

"Not from a bottle. Pour it in a sauceboat. He puts ketchup on my omelet? He should do it so it looks nice."

"He was embarrassed to ask," says the waiter.

"You tell him he doesn't have to be embarrassed to ask for what he wants in a restaurant," says Tell. "He is just American, and he thinks everything is hamburger. Tell him it is good ketchup, too—the slow one or something from television. He will know the name—I forget. Tell him if he wants, we show him the label, like a wine bottle."

After lunch, the staff eats. And Tell, who has just moved to a new apartment, drives me back to visit his wife—in the bright little red Porsche that is his favorite car. The BMW hums when it goes—smoothly and softly, like a woman hums when she's working; the Porsche growls and barks, like one of those little dogs you can't keep quiet. My head snaps back every time he starts and every time he shifts gears.

"I do like fast cars," he says. "We drive home fast. I like to get away an hour, and the help is happy to get me out of there, too. So I am not always standing around. You have to make them happy. You know, sometimes they come in, drink up all the coffee, eat up butter with sweet rolls. I think, 'This stuff is expensive.' Then I remember I worked in Germany for a chef who had such a good memory he knew exactly how much of the roast is left from dinner. If I cut off a little slice, he yells and screams about it. So you know what we did? We would cut off big pieces all through the night. We stick them on the knife and then we stick the knife up under the butcher-block table. You look under the butcher block in the night, you see eight or ten knives up there with a half a pound of meat on each one. We never eat it! We just did it because we hated him. I know all those tricks, and I know it pays to keep the workers happy.

"You look over there . . . is a orphanage, half hidden from trees. Those kids in there got nobody, except some nuns who take care of them. After Thanksgiving I give them a turkey dinner at the restaurant, on the off day. Well, what I am going to do? I have turkey in the restaurant Thanksgiving, and I am going to put leftovers on my menu? Everybody is sick of turkey. That's why they go out to eat. And you see those kids, they get eyes big around like this."

A nice story, almost shyly told and made more interesting by the fact that Tell takes both hands off the wheel to show me how big the kids' eyes get and the Porsche is doing eighty on a curving road.

"HOW WE MET"

"How we met?" says Tell. "I fixed her flat tire."

"I was in Germany for a vacation," says Tell's wife, Janet. "And a friend of mine said her parents ran a little hotel in a spa and I could stay with them. Tell fixed my flat tire in the afternoon. That evening I was sitting around talking to the parents in the bar of the hotel. Some big macho German blond comes in and wants to take me out. I have to explain that I don't know any German and it seems foolish. But he knew the parents, and they said he was just being friendly. Finally, I made him leave his license-plate number and told them to call the police if I wasn't back in two hours. We went out for a drink, and there was Tell again. With his girl friend."

"I know this guy," says Tell. "He is so cheap. So I say everybody we will go to another place and have a drink and dance. Then when we get there I tell the bartender all the drinks are on me."

"The blond guy switched from beer to cognac right away," says Janet.

She is tall, in her early thirties, extremely attractive and, like Tell, an oldest child—both have that independent, almost defiant, air of knowing exactly what they want and how to get it. They seem so suited to each other that it's hard imagining them apart.

"It was just trying to work together," explains Janet.

"So now we don't," says Tell. "I even go to some psychiatrist. He tells me I work hours too long and everybody who can't keep up with me I think is inferior. It's my nature. You know Germans—we are vindictive.

"Anyhow, this guy, the blond back in Germany, gets so drunk I finally say to Janet, 'Look, you can't drive home with him,' and I take everybody home. I drop everybody off, including my girl friend, then I go back to that little hotel and there is Janet still talking to her friend's parents. And I go in. And so."

"It was terrible in this little town, because it was a resort," says Janet, "and I was the rich American lady coming to take their chef away. Because Tell was the big selling point of the main hotel restaurant. One man just walked up on the street and started yelling at me—luckily I couldn't understand a word. Then he spit, right on the ground in front of me, and I understood that. I wasn't rich—I grew up in a city neighborhood and my family owned a sandwich shop—but I did work for the Marriott hotels."

"And when I come to America, 1973, I can't even speak English, so I need Janet to talk to me. Even if you say the same thing, I could understand her and not you. I get a job in the Marriott, six months working for two hundred dollars a week, waiting for regular papers because I have all these offers —thirty thousand, forty thousand dollars. Finally after six months I have to go back to Germany to renew my papers, and I find out—they tell me anyway—somebody is maybe messing up this stuff deliberately so they can keep me working there. I get it straight. I come back and quit the day I get off the plane.

"I go out to work at the Valley Forge Hotel. Then the Barclay in Philadelphia. But at the Barclay I have disagreements with the manager. I walk though the dining room in my chef's uniform and this is the greatest disgrace that ever happened in the history of the Barclay. Then we fight about the menu—he wants stuff like chicken à la king. I tell him I will cook chicken à la king. I will cook anything. I just don't like it on the menu. Then the Marriott calls up. They want me to work for them. I say I will never work for the Marriott no matter what. So they jump the price they pay. I say no. Every day they call back and jump the price some more. Even Germans, how stubborn can we get?

"I am executive chef at the Marriott. We serve six or seven thousand meals a day in the Marriott—more in one day than I serve all week in my restaurant now. We have a conveyor belt for the plates—ten guys stand beside it, one guy puts on mashed potatoes, one puts on ten peas, five carrots, meat gravy. It's crazy. But I learned a lot from the Marriott. They keep food costs down—you have to justify everything, you have to get so many slices from each tomato. Once we get a new manager of the hotel who is trying to save money and he makes me buy unsized and ungraded tomatoes—so he saves seven thousand dollars a year. I tell him that his a false saving but he doesn't believe me. And all of a sudden in the kitchen I am getting the wrong number of slices, and then some of the tomatoes are rotten and so I just save them up in a big stainless-steel tray and once a week I walk into his office and say, 'Here are your tomatoes, man.' We go back to the best tomatoes, and I teach him about false economy and I make an enemy—because he doesn't like being wrong. So I save and work and borrow—and open our own place."

"I stayed a partner even when we separated," says Janet. "Sometimes Tell would try to buy me out and I'd refuse. Sometimes he would back off at the last minute himself. I think we knew—that the restaurant was a part of us. And we couldn't just break it up."

"It is great, America is great," says Tell. "You hear René complain about the food. But he doesn't go back. He can't afford a Jeep in Europe—the taxes on a car are more than a thousand dollars. He can't go fishing every day. To fish in Germany, where all the streams are owned, you pay a hundred twenty-five dollars and you are allowed to fish one afternoon for three hours. Not one afternoon a week. One afternoon and that's all! I couldn't afford my cars, the clothes—it is good here. You work hard—you get something back."

WORKING

Dinner is the hard work of the restaurant. At Erhardt's it starts at six and runs till eleven. The first orders come into the kitchen around six-thirty and the chefs complain wearily but doggedly about the last two or three orders that come in after ten o'clock.

"Ten-fifteen!" says René. "You got table twelve at last?"

"They have another round of drinks," says Johann, with a shrug. "Ordering . . ."

"O.K.! Ordering!" says René happily.

Ted reads off the order. He and Tell and René have all been at the stove nearly four hours, working a kind of sagging zone defense, Tell usually at the big frypans where most things are sautéed. He takes the veal medallions Ted has cut for the last order, flours them, drops them in the pan and puts them on the hottest part of the stove. It smokes and spits. He turns the veal. René has put three long spears of peeled asparagus in a copper serving pan. The partly cooked asparagus is kept underwater in a small pan on the end stove and cooked fresh every half hour or so each night in water that has salt and sugar and a little butter in it. So when the spears come out they have a light shine to them. Tell puts the veal medallions next to the asparagus, fills the pan with the ham and morel stock mix—that becomes *sauce Godard,* pours in an equal amount of heavy cream which boils instantly, gives the frying pan a final shake and pours the sauce over the veal. René adds a quick but carefully decorative dollop of hollandaise on the asparagus. Ted adds rice, puts the serving pan in the broiler oven and takes it out an instant later. The hollandaise has a nice nut-brown glaze, the asparagus is cooked through, the sauce is set on the meat. The whole process takes no more than half a minute.

Sometimes Tell shifts to vegetables or to finishing. Sometimes he walks out into the restaurant and Ted and René work the orders alone. It takes an hour before the characteristic heat flush turns their faces bright red. In two hours their eyes shine from the heat. In the last flurries, toward the end of the dinner rush, their eyes get that red, raw look of staying up all night. After the dinner rush, the eyes go back to normal, the flush disappears—the stoves go off, the kitchen is expertly torn down and the pots turned over to Bob the potman.

"Six bottle Beck beer, very cold and very fast," Tell calls over the phone to the bar. Everybody suddenly seems pale, slow-moving, quiet.

"We drink to the four-legged duck," says Tell. "But so? You have to make every mistake in the kitchen—once. The first day of my apprenticeship, the chef tells me, 'Make potatoes for the night.' I tell him I don't know how, so he kicks me and says, 'You peel potatoes and put them in a pot with salt and put them on the fire. So I did it and half an hour later the kitchen fills with smoke. I didn't put any water in—he didn't tell me. He beats me for this, he beats me for that . . .

"When I was little I didn't like onions. My mother—I don't know if she has some discussions with my father about this—she cooks everything twice. Once for the family, once for me without onions. When you put the food in the pot in the restaurant, you have to taste it first. To see if it's good. I put in onions one time and the chef says, 'First taste.' 'I can't,' I say. 'I don't like onions.' He beats me, he kicks me. I taste the onion and ever since I eat onions all the time. That's what my mother should have done maybe—saved herself all that trouble with the cookings.

"That bastard, I still remember him. Every day he tells me, 'You never make it, you never be a chef.' Finally he knows. *He* never gets his master chef degree. I get to be the youngest master chef in Germany—only twenty-four. He knows . . . that bastard . . . but he teaches me to eat onions."

Erhardt drains his beer and makes a last tour of the restaurant. It is nearly midnight. The dishwashers and potman will be here another hour, Joe and Johann and the waiters another hour and a half. But the kitchen staff is going home. Tippi will be back at nine A.M. René and Ted at eleven. Another day will start.

THE DAY STARTS

The day starts like all the other days the restaurant is open. Tell sits at the big chopping-block table, asking for a minute of quiet. Tippi brings the grapefruit. Vicki brings coffee for everybody. Tippi talks quietly about her hobbies: she takes disco dancing lessons and is learning karate (a green belt and rising). It is a beautiful clear morning, and a soft Chestnut Hill breeze comes through the screen door.

"Okay—only twelve hours to go," says Erhardt, heaving himself suddenly out of the chair and starting on the run. He fills two twenty-gallon pots with water, adds two heads of garlic each and puts them on the stove. He cuts the onions in half to brown them. Ten pounds of butter in another pot to clarify. Asparagus peels in another twenty-gallon pot. Veal bones on to brown. He shifts the butter to a hotter spot on the stove. Wipes the "piano." Shifts the veal bones. Pulls the plastic tubs of stock out of the walk-in box. Three more pots with roux.

"Time to *work*," he says to no one, maybe to the kitchen, maybe to the stove already blazing back at him, giving his face the first heat flush of the morning. "That's why they call me chef!"

TWO

DINER

"We have good coffee," says Richard W. Kubach, Senior, president and founder of the Melrose Diner. He sits across from me in his office at Philadelphia's best-known twenty-four-hour diner. The small desk doubles as a table and has been set for lunch. Mr. Kubach is a hearty and active man of seventy-two, with a trace of a German accent. He says he will never retire, but also insists that he does not work at all hard any more. "My son, Richard Junior, is running the business now—I don't do anything but come into the office and talk to people.

"We have good coffee, as I say. We have a special machine that keeps the water on the ground coffee no longer than four minutes. We have special water, filtered and treated to remove sodium. We use Philadelphia water here only to flush the toilets. We could make our coffee stronger and use less by just letting it sit on the grounds longer—but then you get more things that are bad for you.

"And the taste gets . . . sour. You can drink our coffee without getting stomachaches. But it costs thirty-five cents a cup. Every cup. No refills. I have to charge that if I make coffee this way, and I won't make coffee any way but the best way. People tell me that my coffee is too expensive. Well, it *is* expensive. Coffee costs you two cents a cup at home. But that's because you never figure in all the expenses I have to figure in. And you know what I say? *You* have those expenses too—you have overhead. If you want a cup of coffee in your home, first of all you have to buy the house. You have to pay the gas bill. You have to buy the pot, the cups, the spoon, pay the water bill . . . you have to marry the girl. If you figure up what a cup of coffee costs you, thirty-five cents a cup is not too bad."

As lunch goes on, Mr. Kubach—called simply Dick by most of his employees—tries to explain to an outsider—someone who knows no more about diner food than what he sees on the plate—what it means to run a restaurant that is open twenty-four hours a day, every day but Christmas . . . "Because Christmas I want to be home with my family, and everybody else wants to be home with theirs. We close about eleven A.M. on Christmas Eve and open seven in the morning December twenty-sixth.

"We don't do things the way most other restaurants do them. Now, I am not criticizing other restaurants, and I do not want to hurt anybody else's business. I was very active in the State and the National Restaurant Association, and I think most restaurants are good. Some restaurants are not. I'm going to tell you—you don't have to write this down—I came to this country in 1929 from Germany. I wound up being a dishwasher in a diner on North Broad Street. First dishwasher, then cook, then manager. I always say I learned there how *not* to do things. And I saved my money until I could buy a diner down here, Fifteenth and Snyder Avenue, in 1937. It had been called 'Superior Diner,' but there was nothing superior about it. It was out of business for six months, and all the neighborhood kids had been using it like a toilet. I had to clean it up, and I knew I had to change the name.

"When I was a manager of this other place, there was a brand of tomatoes called Melrose. Only it had the letter M-E-L and then the picture of a rose. I liked that, and I told the sign painter to do it that way and went home. I come back when he is finished and the sign says 'M-E-L-R-O-S-E.' No picture of a rose. I ask him why, and he says he was embarrassed to tell me that he doesn't know how to paint a rose. So, I had a name for my diner. And I wanted a twenty-four-hour diner. And I wanted a good life for myself. So I decided that I had to either work long hours or have good people. I have good people here.

"Now I will tell you something nobody believes except the people who work here. I have always gone home every day at four o'clock in the afternoon. I leave my managers to take care of things. I have never counted my money. I have good people, and I don't need to count it. I had a bad auto accident and was out for a whole year in the hospital in 1970. Nobody in my family was in this diner to take care of it. Just my managers and all the people who work here. Everything went fine. Nobody did anything different. The business went right on growing, like always. Now I will write down some things that we do."

He writes as he talks.

"We never ask the price of anything. We taste it, we test it and we want the best. If there is better food anywhere, at any price, we want to know about it, and we want to buy it. My beef, my lamb, my chicken, my hamburger—which we grind from top sirloin every day—is the best you can buy. Nobody pays more, not any restaurant you can think of. We buy the best, but we buy American-type food. All our bread is Pepperidge Farm, the best American-style bread. This is diner food.

"We use fresh vegetables whenever we can. Asparagus is always fresh. String beans we do not use frozen because we cannot get frozen string beans that we are happy with. Vegetables are steamed, according to our recipes: two minutes for fresh carrots, half a minute for frozen peas. We have to use frozen peas—we can't get good fresh ones. All the vegetables are finished with butter. No margarine. We steam them only two and a half pounds at a time because we do not want vegetables sitting around on a steam table. We have the machinery to cook vegetables fast—there is no need for big pots of things. If you get lamb stew here—a very popular dish—the lamb is cooked with onion and peppers. Potatoes are added next and cooked. Then when you order it, vegetables are cooked separate and added last, so you don't get all soft carrots. You cannot get better vegetables—anywhere.

"We do not buy prepared food. We cut our own steaks to size—we don't buy portion control. We do buy our lamb and beef in chunks and we pay a premium, because we want exactly twelve chunks to a pound. We don't want you to come in one time and get big pieces and the next time little pieces of meat—it has to look the same and taste the same. Everybody here, even the cook who has been here thirty-nine years, works with a recipe card in front of him. Spices are weighed. Cooking time is timed with big photographer's timers that sit everywhere around the kitchen. If a cook takes off, the customer never knows—because his assistant is doing exactly the same thing in exactly the same way. We make our own mayonnaise, our own Russian dressing—our own salad dressing. We have a tossed salad, a diner tossed salad, with not just iceberg—in fact, only a little iceberg—romaine mostly, escarole, curly endive. Nobody pays more for his lettuce than I do. I have one supplier for vegetables, one for meat—I do not even want bargains. I want the best.

"We do all our own baking. We employ eight bakers. We sell fourteen thousand apple pies a year. We make them up fresh every day. But we do not bake them in the morning and then all the bakers go home. That way you have soggy pies at the end of the day. Pies are made up, then put in the freezer, then baked as we need them. We plan to run out of pies at lunch, so you have fresh pies when you come in for dinner. The pies are baked, then we turn them over—we don't want pies that stick to the bottom of the pan. They sit on refrigerated shelves after they cool—your pie is never more than two hours or so out of the oven. Danish we make ourselves, bake until just underdone and then freeze. We bake them off one tray at a time, twelve Danish—your Danish is never more than half an hour from the oven, and almost all the time it is five or ten minutes.

"We make sure our people are happy. I was a dishwasher. I was a cook. I always say, a dishwasher has to pay the same as you do for a pair of shoes. There is no discount just because he is a dishwasher. And he has to live, just like everybody else. Minimum wage is—three something an hour. I don't want a

minimum-wage dishwasher. I want a five-dollar-an-hour dishwasher. Minimum wage for waitresses is much lower because they get tips, a dollar something. Our waitresses get three-fifty an hour plus tips. And the tips are divided equally among the waitresses and the short-order cook—so everybody is equally interested in getting the good food to the customer.

"We have a five-day week—not many other restaurants do. Most have six days. We have a seven-and-a-half-hour day. We may be the only restaurant that doesn't have a ten- or twelve-hour day. After seven and a half hours, you are paid time and a half. Holidays, time and a half. If you come in an extra day because we need you, you are doing us a favor—time and a half. We have a pension, we have Blue Cross–Blue Shield. And each manager each week makes up the schedule for the people working for him. He is closest to those people and his job is keeping them happy. So if you want a day off, you just write it down on a piece of paper and he makes sure first. If at all possible, you get that day off. You don't need any reasons.

"I always say, if there is somebody unhappy, we want to know why. You know, nobody ever makes enough money. Nobody. So if you start out with a job and you don't make enough money and besides you are unhappy, then you're *really* unhappy. At least we can make sure that our people aren't unhappy because of us. I tell all my managers, I tell all the people who work here—we need you more than you need us. A good worker can always get a job, and these are the best workers. We make sure to keep them. We have a twenty-five-year club. There are waitresses like Betty Baillie and Jean Di Elsi who have been here—Betty thirty-nine years, Jean thirty-five years. My general manager just retired last year after forty-three years—he had been with me since I opened.

"We value our employees and so we keep them. You know, if the dishwasher quits—who winds up doing the dishes? It can't be the chef—he has a job. The manager has a job. The general manager has a job. The only one without a job around here is me—and I don't want to wash dishes. You think I am joking. I know of a place right now—a friend called me on the phone and said, 'Who do you think is washing the dishes last night and tonight? The owner.' You know what I said? I said, *'It serves him right!* Maybe he will learn to keep his dishwasher happy now.'"

A GLASS OF WATER
A TOUR OF THE WORKS

From the front, the Melrose is a medium-size diner—ten booths and a long counter. Seating capacity, 107. Every year *one million* people eat here. To handle that volume, there is a huge kitchen behind the eating area, at least twice as large. Beyond the kitchen is another area, at least as large as the front seating part, which is refrigeration, storage, receiving and garbage. Under the whole building runs a basement filled with airconditioning ducts, storage, the cake decorating department, water filters, heaters, special sewage equipment. I take a tour with Kubach and his son, a graduate of Cornell University with a degree in hotel and restaurant administration, who is obviously as delighted with his father as his father is with him.

"We will start downstairs, in the basement. It is a little messy now because we have installed new air conditioning. But you will see what it is like. First, before we go down, here is the loading dock. Now we refrigerate our garbage."

Richard opens the door of a refrigerator and shows me the ten garbage cans, all neatly covered, inside.

"It keeps down flies," says Richard Junior. "You can see the door at the back—which opens to the outside. The garbage man never comes in the restaurant. He takes the stuff out. We clean it down. We also refrigerate our towels—we use lots of towels for wiping up because we're always cleaning, and you don't refrigerate the dirty ones, they get sour and smell. You can actually find restaurants where they have maggots in the old towels. The garbage goes every morning, the towels go every morning."

"The loading dock is not air-conditioned," says Richard Senior. "That is the only place where employees work that is not.

The dressing rooms are air-conditioned. The kitchen is air-conditioned. We want people comfortable."

I take a tour through the spotless cellar and admire more machines than I ever knew existed. A special heater that warms the walkway and steps outside to melt snow in the winter; a water softener for good sudsing water in the washing sinks; a filter so there can be softened and filtered water in the dishwashing machine—because otherwise mineral residue in Philadelphia water will clog the sprays.

"But you can't have softened water for coffee or soups—they wouldn't taste right. So we have plain filtered water, taste-treated to remove all traces of chlorine. A glass of water in the Melrose is different than a glass of water in any other restaurant," says Richard Senior. "Now look at this special machine, which you have never seen anywhere else."

A collection of pipes that looks like the engine room of a boat, sunk in a cement well set in the floor.

"There a problem with the sewers in South Philadelphia from time to time," says Richard Junior. "And sometimes the system flushes back—people go down to their cellar and discover that the sewage is spilling back up into the house."

"We can't have this," says Richard Senior. "So this is a machine that flushes the sewage back into the sewers. Thirty-horsepower pumps. No matter how bad the flooding gets anywhere else, this basement is always perfectly dry . . . Now you have to see our art department."

CAKES AND ROSES

The art department—an air-conditioned cubicle in the center of the basement—is where the cakes are decorated. Kurt Bundschuh, the head baker of the Melrose, is in charge of decoration. There are only a few designs the Melrose will do. All icings are butter icings. All cakes are baked fresh the day they are sold. All decorations are edible.

"We're one of the few bakeries that still do our own roses," says Richard Junior. "Each rose is done by hand."

"A baker just stopped in last month and asked us where we buy our roses—because most places get frozen or else preservative roses for the top of the cakes," says Richard Senior. "He could not believe it when I said we make our own."

"We sell between thirty and forty cakes a day," says Kurt, a muscular man in his fifties, with a German accent of his own. He demonstrates a rose as he talks—squeezing colored butter cream out of a pastry bag onto a tiny dome base he calls a nail —eight or ten little swirls—and he lifts the rose off with the point of a big kitchen knife.

"We tell people order two days in advance, but sometimes we do emergencies," says Kurt. "Actually, we do a lot of emergencies. A lot of marriages are happier because the husband stops in here when he forgot the birthday or the anniversary. The night manager knows how to put the name on with decorating gel, and you would be surprised how often he does it—sometimes two or three emergency cakes a night. Each day when we are finished, we take all the utensils, put them through the dishwasher, soak them in sterilizing solution, put them through the dishwater again to get the sterilizer off—and then they go in the refrigerator. Here, let me show you." Kurt opens his refrigerator and takes out three or four long-handled pastry spatulas.

"You see those handles, how they are bleaching white? That is from being sterilized every day. No bacteria. You can eat off this floor. I don't mean the way a good housewife says it. I mean we clean these floors with antiseptic solution every day when we are finished. These floors are as clean as our plates. You can eat off them!"

"I always say it," says Richard Kubach Senior.

CONTROL

"Control," says Paul Tierney, general manager of the Melrose. Paul is a tall man with closely cropped white hair that gives him the look of one of those very humane but very efficient colonels you sometimes used to find in the Army before it fell apart during the war in Vietnam. The very best kind of officer —if you do your job. "Control. Equipment. Talent. You look around this kitchen."

It is 7 A.M. The first shift of the new day has taken over from the night crew. Breakfast is already in full swing—there are, as always, at least sixty people in the restaurant: morning workers, guys with extra jobs with dreamy, overworked looks on their faces, enjoying their one luxury—breakfast. The cooks are already beginning to get ready for lunch. Veal and lamb go in the oven to brown before they stew. Marion Moses, the kitchen manager, thirty-nine years at the Melrose, flips the specially designed menu card to the recipe for chicken soup:

Take 25 lbs chicken necks and backs.
Add water to fill 40-gallon tureen.
Add carrots, onions, tomatoes.
Cook 2 hours.
Draw off 22 gallons stock.
Discard vegetables.
Add dice of carrots, onions, celery.
Cook 20 minutes.
Before serving, steam peas and string beans to add at last minute.

"Now you might think this is almost comical, a man with thirty-nine years experience following a recipe—but that's an element of control," says Paul. "We want the soup to be the same every day. Mo is going to be off this weekend—how many restaurants do you know where the chef can take off for the weekend? Of course, we do not call Mo the chef. Nobody in this kitchen wears a tall white hat. We have managers, cooks, assistants. Mo's assistant will just take over this weekend, make the chicken soup exactly the same way—and nobody will know the difference. Mr. Kubach Senior always says, 'We want a system where we don't miss a person when they're out.' And the customer shouldn't miss them either.

"You look at this kitchen—it has tile floor, plaster walls, lots of stainless-steel grating and ductwork to take the grease out and for air conditioning. What do you hear?"

"Nothing," I say.

"That's right," says Paul. "All these hard surfaces to bounce sound around and you hear nothing. The machinery is in the basement or up on the roof. The people are working. The short-order cooks call in when they want more bacon or scrapple or ham. But they call once and they get it. No yelling. No running around. People don't have to move from where they're working in here. Things are designed too well. We have big refrigerators against the back wall. We have tiny refrigerators, big enough to hold the morning's supplies in these drawers down here—right under the steamers. Everything goes into the preparation space for the short-order cooks through this one window. Nobody has to walk all over the place to do their job.

"Now here is how our hamburgers are made. Foster McKnight has this job every morning. He starts off with top sirloin. We bring the sirloin in fresh every day and it goes into the freezer to firm it up a bit so it cuts better. Then it goes into a big machine that is just an industrial version of your Cuisinart at home. When it comes out of there, it's not like hamburger—it's more like cut meat, it has a different texture. Then it goes through a regular grinder to give it the hamburger texture. If we just ground it twice, it would be too much for hamburger. We've experimented and tested and tasted all different kinds of grinds, and this is the best we could find. Then it goes into a machine that stamps out each one of the hamburgers.

"We don't want aged beef for hamburger, because we're dealing with ground meat. Grinding meat speeds up the aging process, and, especially in the fat, you can taste that age very quickly. So all our hamburger is slaughtered the same day it's delivered to us. We buy only kosher-killed top sirloin for our hamburger—that's the only way we can be absolutely certain it's same-day slaughtered. Nobody else has hamburger like this. Nobody else pays what we do. My wife can't get hamburger like this—*you* can't get hamburger like this. Which is as it should be—anybody buying the volume we buy should be able to demand better meat than ordinary people can buy. And we will pay a premium to get what we want.

"I want you to look around and notice how we buy things. We buy butter in one-pound blocks. I could get the same butter at half the price if I bought it in bulk—but this way, everything is premeasured, everything is controllable. And we don't have big tubs sitting around collecting bacteria. That's the way we do it. We do not make Italian food or any ethnic kind of food. But we do have a side dish of what we call 'bite-size spaghetti'—actually it's *rotelli*. We buy it in one-pound packages. La Fara. Imported. The best we can buy.

"We pay a premium for our uniforms. You will never see a cook or a waitress walking around with a uniform that has stitches in it to repair it. You will never see even a towel with patchwork on it, even if it's just used to wipe tables. I pay extra for that. I get the new towels. We buy California strawberries only—and we get them ripe. Look."

Paul holds up a tray of the first really ripe berries I have seen all spring, each one two inches across and purple as a bruise.

"We have to pay for this. Florida and Mexican berries are just not good enough. Local berries from Jersey are very good, but they never get big enough—we have to have our size.

"We have a dishwashing machine—I want you to look at this machine."

It is, like everything in the kitchen, stainless steel, with a semicircular conveyor belt that carries the dishes out of the washer and back around to almost the same place they started.

"This machine is designed so that one man can work it. Mr. Kubach Senior designed this himself—like he designed the coffee urn, the kitchen, the whole place—working with models in his living room. When we're busy, two men can fit in the space, and two men are all we ever need. The dishwasher, like everybody else, doesn't have to do a lot of walking around. He's got a hard job, and we want to make it as easy as possible. Mr. Kubach always says that we need good people more than they need us." He stops and grins. "You've been hearing a lot of what Mr. Kubach always says, I guess."

I have, I admit.

"We all pick it up: *A dishwasher has to spend as much*

money for a pair of shoes as you do . . . We never ask the price of anything . . . We always want the best . . . Nobody ever quits . . . It's all part of the Melrose. Once people fit in with us, it's true—we spoil them. We will do anything to keep good people.

"Now, all the silverware is washed three times. First, it's soaked in antiseptic solution and scrubbed with a brush by hand. Then it goes through the dishwasher—triple wash, sterilizing temperature. Then the man has to pick the silver out of the trays. Now there's nothing wrong with that silver—it's as clean as it can be. But it isn't sterile. He's been touching the part that you eat with when he picks it up. So he puts the silver in plastic containers, eating side up, and runs it through the dishwasher—all over again. Now it's sterile. And he turns it over into those other plastic containers, so it is handle up. When the waitresses take the silver out, they take it by the handle and put it in the bins under the counter—nobody's hands have touched the part you eat with since it has been sterilized. You have to keep after sanitation that way—or you lose control.

"We blanch all the celery, thirty seconds, in boiling water," says Paul. "You can't taste the difference once we get it cold again—but studies have shown that celery has a very high bacteria content. It sounds funny, but it's true—and we want to make sure we keep bacteria count down . . . to the minimum.

"Every time the Cuisinart is used it is broken down by the man who uses it—cleaned, soaked in Lo-Bax—that's our sterilizing solution—and then put back together. After you've done whatever you're doing, the next man should be able to come along and use that same machine—and never realize what it is you were making. Now, here's another machine.

"This is a silver burnisher." Paul flips it open to show the inside, full of tiny steel ball bearings and a pink sludge that looks like semidissolved silver polish. "We used to have silver plate but went over to stainless years ago. But all our flatware is still burnished every night. It's put in here and tumbled around with all these little balls and thinned-down polish—and it makes our knives and forks and spoons shine. People say this isn't necessary—but ask the waitresses around here. If they miss a spoon one night and don't burnish it, you can pick it out across the room. *I* can pick it out, and the manager can pick it out, too. That's his job."

"Everything has to meet our standards. You know, if you have a good restaurant, you have a lot of competition. If you have a very good restaurant, there isn't quite so much competition. So if you raise your standards higher and higher, you eventually get to the point where you have no competition. That's what we are trying."

"That sounds like one of the things Mr. Kubach Senior says," I say.

"It's one of the things he *always* says," says Paul.

MY FATHER

"My father," says Richard Kubach Junior, "is an unusual man. He always says that in some restaurants the owner is the heartbeat. If the owner gets sick, the restaurant falls apart. He didn't want that, so he had to have a restaurant where the people who worked in the restaurant were the heartbeat. And they are."

We are sitting at a corner of the counter, at Betty Baillie's station. Betty is a small woman with a slight Scottish burr, seventy-five years old, who still works at least three days a week at the Melrose. She kids with the customers and brings food and clears as we talk. It takes me several minutes to realize that half the people are not ordering any food.

"Well, don't *I* know what they want by now?" asks Betty Baillie. "This one is a troublemaker."

"Wait." A portly cop sits down and begins to talk quickly. "Not the usual. Salad instead. Only *no* cucumbers."

"No *cucumbers?* What do you want me to do, pick them out? They're all made up in the kitchen."

"They said you'd pick them out, Betty," says the cop in a mock-hurt voice.

"Now look around," says Richard. "The stripping around

the ceiling looks just like an ordinary diner. But it's actually hiding ductwork that runs all along the walls. Under your feet, at the base of the counter, is more ductwork. We have a negative air pressure in here—air is constantly coming in from the ceiling and moving back toward the kitchen. There are more vents over the preparation room forcing air into the room. And big vents over the stoves taking air out. You can't hear anything, not even a hum—because all the motors are on the roof. But every time the door opens, air comes in—you never smell food cooking outside the Melrose. Air is constantly going away from the customer—you never smell food cooking no matter where you sit to eat. We have such a good system of air flow that we hardly ever have anybody complain about smoking—though lots of our customers smoke. The system just dispenses with it.

"The booths are designed by my father—they're very large, but divided in half, so there's no trouble accommodating a big party and a couple doesn't take up a whole booth by themselves. There's a formica panel that comes out to divide the booth in half—because we don't want people to touch feet . . . or anything . . . under the table. Late at night, when different people have been out clubbing—that might be a problem. The table has a metal tray underneath to hold a towel to wipe it clean. We don't have busboys. The waitress comes over, wipes the table, and takes your order. In other restaurants, a busboy has to walk across the room, pick up the towel, walk over to the table, wipe and walk back to replace the towel. We dispense with all that work.

"I don't know if you ever have trouble getting a check after you've finished eating. You never have trouble in the Melrose. When the waitress brings your order, she puts the check beside you. When she brings coffee and dessert, she totals the check the minute she puts the dessert on the table. As soon as you're finished, you can leave. Most people don't notice when she does that—though they do notice that they don't have the irritation of looking for a waitress and asking for a bill. That's what we like to do—be efficient, but be so quiet about it that you don't notice it."

As he talks, Betty Baillie has brought the cop his salad. "Any cucumbers?" he asks. "I hate cucumbers."

"I'll give you a nickel for every one you find," says Betty.

And the cop searches through and finds one—a tiny sliver that is undeniably a cucumber.

"Where's my nickel?" says the cop.

"Wait here," says Betty, who goes to bring over the short-order cook. "Look what he wants a nickel for."

"I believe he brought his own cucumber in his pocket, just to get that nickel," says the cook.

"I hate cucumbers," says the cop. "But I have to have salads to lose weight. I got to lose thirty pounds."

"You'll never lose thirty pounds," says Betty.

"I lost ten already," says the cop proudly.

"Where?" says Betty. "In your feet?"

The laughing cop eats up the chunk of apple pie that Betty brings over without being asked—his usual dessert.

"Why not?" he says. "At least I got skinny feet."

SATURDAY NIGHT AND SUNDAY MORNING, PART ONE: LARRY PREDICTS

Larry Tentarelli is the assistant general manager of the Melrose, working with Paul Tierney. Still in his thirties, black-haired, he has the kind of aggressive friendliness that is best described by the memos he puts up on the tiny bulletin board between the kitchen and the preparation room:

> GIRLS: Please ask the customers if they want butter with the pancakes and please don't bring more than one pat of butter with the rolls. We are not trying to be chintzy with the butter. Give them anything they ask for. But there is no sense in senseless waste. Larry.

I sit with Larry at the end of the morning shift—3 P.M.—drinking my tenth or twelfth cup of coffee of the day, watching him watch the room. I'm getting used to that casual manager alertness now—I realize that while he's talking to me, kidding with the waitresses, saying hello to the dozen or so customers who know him by name, he is also constantly scanning the room.

"You're going to stay through the late shift? Saturday night and Sunday morning? It's a good shift—eleven P.M. to seven A.M. Now, you know we get a lot of people in here who are steady customers. There are people whose every bite that goes into their mouths comes from the Melrose—I'm serious. They're in here for breakfast, for lunch, for dinner, and if they want a late-night snack, this is where they come for it. Now, you take people who are out clubbing. They're the same people —but they're feeling a little good. We don't get too many people who are rowdy, because we know how to control that.

"I'll tell you what the crowd is like. Just the other day, I'm riding on a trolley and these two girls get on and sit in front of me. One says how she hates her job and she can't wait to get home and hates her home and can't wait to get out with her boyfriend and hates her boyfriend and can't wait to get home. The usual. The other one says, 'Don't go home. Go to the Melrose.' Then she starts saying how the best part of Saturday night isn't going out, isn't her boyfriend, isn't the club—it's the Melrose after. I'm sitting right behind them, taking all this in. She tells her how the lights are bright so the older girls' wrinkles show up. And how she makes sure to put on new makeup. And how it's a good place to meet somebody who might ask you out later. And she's right. I'm serious.

"And I'll tell you another thing. My wife is from South Philly and when I was still going with her—before we got married—I knew lots of people down here. There are girls who don't go out on Saturday night. They go to bed nine, ten o'clock and *set the alarm* for two A.M.! They get up, spend three quarters of an hour getting dressed and another half an hour putting on makeup—and then go over to the Melrose when the clubs let out at around three. The other girls've been out and around, and here they are, fresh makeup, big smile, bright eyes. And they go to the ladies room twelve times an hour, showing off the body. Guys think they've been out clubbing and look so good because they look so good . . . Not a bit of it. But there's a lotta guys go away from here saying, 'I never knew Donna was so pretty,' and give her a call the next day. You watch and you'll see everything I tell you."

WAIT!! EVERYBODY WHO KNOWS TALKS ABOUT AN APPLE PIE

The second greatest truth of the Melrose—right up there next to the fact that a dishwasher has to pay the same price for a pair of shoes as you or I—is the fact that the apple pie has to be the best there is. The Apple Pie Story was told to me at least once by each and every person I interviewed—so often that I stopped taking it down and just wrote *Apple Pie Again,* then *Apple,* then simply a scrawled *AP*.

"You take pretty fast shorthand," said Larry Tentarelli, as he told the story of the apple pie. But I don't—so I can't tell the story his way. The most complete way was from Richard Kubach Senior.

"Our apple pie *has* to be the best there is. We are constantly testing. We know the competition, and we know our product. We want the best. We use canned apples, because we want them perfect and we want them always the same. But we don't like the way apples are canned—there is too much sugar in them. So first we test, we make our pies with different kinds of apple. Rome Beauty, New York State Delicious, Winesap, Stayman. We invite canners down and they eat our pies so they know what we want. We test the pH value—for acidity. My son Richard is very good at this—he learned all about it in Cornell. We finally decide on Golden Delicious from western Pennsylvania, and when the harvest is coming in we go out to the Pittsburgh area to the canner. They mix a batch for us to test—pH again, tasting again. We finally decide on what is right for us. They close down the production line, clean the machines, then they spend two hours canning apples the way *we* want it. And we have all those cases of apples in storage—our pies will be exactly the same every day, each day, until the next harvest."

Paul Tierney stands with me as the baker puts the apples in the crusts, telling the same story about the canning.

"Now, we can these apples very dry, so we can add juice, and we add apple juice. We tested apple juice and we tested water. You can talk to cooks and you will find at least as many who say that water is fine and apple juice is an expense that doesn't make much difference. I tasted these pies both ways and I know it doesn't make much difference. I'm not saying *no* difference. You can make a very good apple pie with water. But the old man—Mr. Kubach Senior—he says we use apple juice. That's the Melrose way. It *has* to be the best."

The apples, dark with juice and spices, are sitting in a large tub—the largest amount of any one food item I have ever seen at the Melrose, and I ask Paul how come the pies aren't made and spiced individually.

"You mean just dump in the spices and the apple juice and then dump the apples in the pie? Don't you know that the spices have to have time to *flavor* the apples? We can't just do these things like some production-line bakery. These apples and spices have been sitting together overnight until the flavor takes. Our pies *have* to be the best."

Richard Junior shows me the machine that rolls out a piecrust in two quick actions—like putting clothes through an old-fashion wringer washer. He tells the story of the canning (again), then says, "You see the man over there scoring a big tray of what looks like butter? It isn't butter. It's a mixture of butter and lard that we make ourselves because we don't like those plastic shortenings for our pies. We freeze the mix, then score it, then mix it in, very roughly, with the dough. We make three kinds of pie dough—top dough, bottom dough and shell dough for custard pies. Bottom dough and shell dough are almost alike—the shortening is very thoroughly mixed in, because if you have fat that's not worked in, it'll drip out the bottom, and that's what causes sticking. We can't have that, as I'm sure everybody has told you."

He opens a refrigerator to show me a batch of top dough—big squares of shortening about an inch across show all through the dough.

"We take a section of this top dough, shape it, run it through the machine in just two swipes and it's crust," says Richard Junior. "If you have a cookbook, a good cookbook with a recipe for flaky dough, the instruction will tell you not to work the dough too much. We work it so little that it *has* to be the flakiest you can get."

GOOD MANAGEMENT

Paul Tierney explains Melrose policy. "We don't have a minimum on our menu. You see that some places—five dollars a person during the dinner hour. We don't have to do things like that. First of all, people come here to eat, and they can do what they want. We have a high turnover. Sometimes you might have somebody come in and just not leave. Well, you have to deal with that on an individual basis—every person is different and every person has to be treated different. That's what our policy is—and it works better than some hard and fast rule. It's better management.

"Like the telephone. We want our people to be able to get personal phone calls and make personal calls during working hours. We have working mothers here. And working fathers, too. They want to know how the kids are doing. And there are lots of reasons besides kids to use a phone—all important. But we don't want people conducting their entire social lives on the restaurant phone. And sometimes—mostly with younger people—we have to tell them that. We don't want them *not* to make calls. We don't want them not to make *social* calls. What's more important when you're young? What we want is for things to work out. Things do.

"Let me tell you the story of Kurt Bundschuh, our head baker. This is a man who was trained to be a baker in Germany—started at nine years old in the apprentice system and has been a baker all his life. About five years ago he started getting sick—really sick. He lost a lot of time. He saw a lot of doctors. Finally, they said to him, 'Kurt, you've become allergic to flour.' Here was a man in his late forties—had never done anything else in his life. He couldn't be around flour. He actually started looking around for some new kind of job—he couldn't just go on welfare. He was—well, you can imagine how you'd feel. Old Mr. Kubach just talked to him and talked to him. He said, 'Kurt, we'll work something out.' He did. He built the Art Department down in the basement, where Kurt is in a completely air-conditioned and flour-free environment. Only completed cakes. Kurt is still the head baker. He stays away when the flour is being mixed, but he will be upstairs again and again all through the day to check on the cakes and the pies and rice pudding and French toast and Danish—all his responsibility. The product is still the same, the restaurant is lucky to have Kurt—you know that we need a good person more than a good person needs us—and Kurt's health is fine. And he is now training his son to work with him and take over some day. That's good management."

SATURDAY NIGHT AND SUNDAY MORNING, PART TWO: IN THE POURING RAIN

Let me do the Melrose, I thought—all I have to do is sit on a stool Saturday night and Sunday morning and describe the first thousand people who walk through the door. Catholic high school girls in every stage of life from subteen tank top to upswept redheaded grandmom—all of them infinitely desirable. Guys in tank tops, tattoos, three-piece suits, satin nylon jackets that say BISHOP NEUMANN if the guy drives a truck and UNITED BROTHERHOOD OF TEAMSTERS if he is a bartender at an any-sex discotheque. White, Black, straight, gay, drunk, sober—and all the stages between those words that seem like mutually exclusive categories to people who've never been to the Melrose on Saturday night. Let me do the Melrose, I thought—even in the pouring rain. It's very strange.

That was a couple weeks ago—before I learned about apple pie and steamed vegetables or even thought about the shoes of the dishwasher. It is, however, pouring rain when I finally sit down, with another cup of coffee, in a corner of the counter at the Melrose, Saturday night. I have had another look at the Melrose coffee urn, which has spigots on both sides —so the short-order cooks can have coffee whenever they want it—and a special pressure gauge on the side. "Because," Paul Tierney says, "this is South Philly and in the summertime the kids turn on the hydrants—water pressure drops. This machine works completely automatically and times the amount of water that comes in—so we have to have equipment to keep our pressure up no matter how the pressure dips around us. Otherwise, we get less water—and different coffee. Which we can't have."

I am resolved that this will be the last of all the secret secrets of good management, but Paul tells me yet one more.

"You can't be too careful about water. You know that we heat the water for the toilets in the ladies room?"

"You *heat* the water for the *toilets?* Why in God's name would you do a thing like that?"

"Well, if you use plain water, there's a difference in temperature with the air of the room, and the bowl has a tendency to sweat and feel damp. You know that happens at home, especially in the summertime. Well, this is a public place—something like that just doesn't look right. We can't have it at the Melrose. Warm water keeps those bowls nice and dry."

I sit down with Victor Klein, manager of the 4-to-11-P.M. shift as he is about to leave. Victor is a tall big-boned man with a shock of white hair and a big-boned look that is too athletic to be heavy.

"If that was ordinary diner coffee you'd be dead by now," laughs Victor and fills me in on what is happening. "George Hurst, the eleven-P.M.-to-seven-A.M. manager is at the door—he'll be there most of the night, sort of looking people over and making sure they pay when they leave. People who've had a couple drinks sometimes think it's fun to jump a check. The coffee machines have already been torn down and scrubbed—pipes and spigots brushed, everything soaked in Lo-Bax. That happens three times a day so that coffee residue doesn't build up.

"Now I want you to eat and start with our bean soup. It's

made entirely from white Great Northern beans, ham, onions —plus filtered and taste-treated water, of course. And you've never tasted bean soup like this. Plus, I am going to let you taste it plain first and then taste it gourmet style."

Two sixteen-year-olds, not drunk but yawning from beer, sit beside me. One wears a white, ribbed undershirt and a tattoo of a rose on his naked shoulder. The other has a T-shirt printed with a street sign that says ELVIS PRESLEY BOULEVARD, MEMPHIS TENNESSEE. Both were born ten years after "Love Me Tender" was first forgotten. The kids both order by number—"CB two, medium rare"—without looking at the menu. Like all the night people, they like to show off the fact that they've memorized every item of food available at the Melrose.

I try the bean soup straight, and then Victor pours in a quarter teaspoon of vinegar—which smooths out all the saltiness and gives the very good soup a very good new flavor.

"That's the gourmet style, and the best way to eat our—yo, buddy, you're not going to sleep." Victor touches the kid on the tattoo the minute his head hits his arms, and the kid's head comes up with a start.

"No, Victor, sorry," says the kid. "I'm done and I'm leaving."

He walks quickly and gingerly to the door, apologizing again as he goes.

"You have to keep right on top of that," says Victor. "One of the things I hate to see is people falling asleep. You've been to all-night diners where that happens? The only thing to do is keep on top of it, never lose control, exercise your authority, get them out. They know. And they know me, even if I'm never around on this shift. That kid'll be back in Monday, after school, polite and quiet as you please."

The kids are getting less sleepy and a little more beery. They mix in with a crowd of husbands and wives out after the late movie, who sit beside each other at the counter—so long married they're in the habit of eating in silence. The very youngest and the very oldest of the wives let their husbands know it's time to go by resting their heads, just for a second, on their husbands' shoulder.

The kids act like kids at camp—spearing whole slices of ham up from their plates and eating them slowly, in five or six bites, snapping at the meat in midair. Except when the waitresses pass, of course, when they sit up straighter and act nice. All the boys in tank tops do not have dates and talk about girls. All the boys with girls wear South Philly's newest style—looks something like an unblocked and unshaped Eisenhower jacket, made of nubby tweed or white rayon. They talk about English class:

"He told my mother at parents' night he caught me cheating twice and so I told her, what do you want, no cheating or summer school, right?"

"Wait, Boswell."

"There's no Father Boswell, Frankie. What's wrong with you?"

"No, *Boswell*. We read him. Here—I got it written down." A kid with black hair cropped thickly around his head, black shadow at the back of his neck where the hair has been shaved, fishes in his wallet. "Somebody asks Johnson about this book and says, 'What, have you read it through?' 'No sir! No one reads a book through!' So see, even Johnson cheated."

"Frankie, you're letting them get to ya if you're reading this stuff."

"Only you'll be the one in summer school, and I'll be making construction money working with *your* uncle . . ."

The girls coming in are getting older—more baggies and less designer jeans. Eyelids marked with so much makeup so long ago that it has slipped sidewise, somehow, giving them the look of those mass-produced, hand-painted statues of the Virgin Mary, where the black eye paint is never quite exactly on the plaster eye rim.

A guy in a Hawaiian shirt outside his pants—no buttons buttoned at all. Nineteen. Dark glasses. Hair that crinkles back off his face in waves; no part. A toothpick.

"Hey," says Frankie, who reads Boswell. "The Guinea Prince."

Lots of shoulder slapping.

Late-night young marrieds. The husbands in three-piece suits bought when they were five pounds lighter, hair combed across their heads and blown dry to cover the receding hairline. Nobody except the married men wear suits. All of them take off the jackets when they sit down to eat. About 50 percent of the shirts are short sleeved. Wives bright and pretty, dressed in five-year-old styles they still fit comfortably into. No baggies except on single girls. No shoes without high heels on any of the women. Black couples with the men dressed in exactly the same three-piece suits as everybody else, the women wearing exactly the same loopy earrings—except that they're in their forties instead of their thirties.

Girls parade to the ladies room, just like Larry said they would, showing the body. Shoes with high heels and almost without any visible straps to keep them on their feet. Double-knit slacks that show taut, arched seams of panties underneath.

There is a crowd by the door now waiting for seats. George Hurst is trying to keep them in line. Two A.M.—I begin to recognize some faces. The owners of Wildflowers restaurant who stop in often after they close "because we love diner food." The entire staff of at least two different Chinese restaurants.

A guy butters his toast with the intent and casual grace of the very, very drunk. He wears a plaid sport shirt and Windbreaker—ordinary blue-collar work clothes—and almost drops, but miraculously saves, every third forkful of egg. It's kind of like watching one of those jugglers who pretend to be clumsy—only in reverse. Guys in their fifties, out without their wives, who stop in, order pancakes and cough around their cigarettes. Guys with dark chino dungarees, shirts with tiny alligators and hard bulblike bellies—who all come in together and all get in an argument about the best way to repair a tubeless tire. Guys with gray sideburns and black Grecian Formula hair, no ties, open shirts, suits with no vests. They come with women who have at least two colors of makeup on their eyelids and at least three rings on each hand. They have pink cotton-candy hair and big earrings in loops or circles or triangles or squares. Chains with crosses of all kinds, including the Maltese and the Lorraine. Stars of David, sometimes alone, sometimes with crosses, once (I think) with a golden sliver that is the moon of Islam. Dog tags in beaten gold with a diamond dotting the "i" in Terri. Razor blades in beaten gold with a diamond at each end of the center slits. A cast gold pennant shaped like the boot of Italy. Gold hands with the first and little finger extended, to ward off the evil eye. An ankh.

The women laugh in line at the take-out counter.

"We never see you down the club anymore."

"This is the first I've been out since the baby."

"We see your husband, though."

"You can have my husband. I got what I wanted from him."

"You can have *my* husband. I got him asleep outside right now, dead drunk in the car. I never get what I want from him."

A man alone in a tuxedo, a waiter or musician, very weary and sober, lights a cigarette, leans his elbow on the counter, his thumb against his right temple, and closes his eyes, slowly and luxuriously. A Black family with a ten- or twelve-year-old, very proud to be up this late and to be wearing a white poplin raincoat that is brand-new—standing up very straight inside that raincoat. By now, only the husbands have sideburns. Every male under thirty has shaved off his sideburns—all the way up to the top of his ear, like Olivier did playing Hamlet. A new South Philly style has been born while no one was watching. Many of the young guys have deliberately neglected to shave for three days—just to look macho enough for Saturday night at the Melrose. And possibly each other.

A guy in a gray tweed slouch jacket, blue chamois T-shirt, white chinos, two little button gold earrings in one ear. A beautiful sixteen-year-old who wears her hair in a single braid that reaches down her back to her waist, plus a NO NUKES button on her plastic see-through raincoat. Two Black women who come in together and have peroxide hair—which turns the dark-skinned one's hair a bright bilious orange, and the light-skinned one's a pale pastel beige.

Suddenly, a whole group of girls in light, crisp dresses, with bright eyes, smiling faces—so clearly happy they seem to be trying to flirt the ketchup out of the ketchup bottles. They walk back and forth to the ladies room. They say hello to everybody —even to the guys with the macho three-day growths—they stop just long enough to say, "Oh no, you have to have a book or something. I never write my number on a *napkin.*" Then get slowly and shyly coaxed into writing their number on the napkin.

Four A.M. Still raining. Women by themselves. The better they're dressed, the younger they are and the more likely their mascara is to be cried into streaks. It's always the dark night of somebody's soul. At any booth where there are still married couples, they are in groups of six or eight—and at least one wife begins to laugh and laugh but won't tell anybody— especially not her husband—what she's thought of that's so funny. A guy with a thick-napped sport coat, furry beard and a gold tooth, so muscular that he has to reach out in front of him one arm at a time, like a swimmer, to loosen his arms in the sleeves when he sits down.

"Jeanne with an *e,*" says his girl friend, leaning over my shoulder as I write. "Put me in whatever you're writing, even if it's just a poem."

Her boyfriend is the guy with the gold tooth. Her girl friend has bright red-fox hair, no makeup at all, "because I'm too beautiful to bother," she says matter-of-factly.

"Come on back here, Jeanne."

"We're talking about potatoes," says Jeanne.

"I dreamed of potatoes," says the redhead, who really is too beautiful for makeup. "We were talking about potatoes, and suddenly I could see everything clear. Everything. The world. You know, everything was clear. Very profound—for a dream."

The gold razor blades are closer to free form now— trapezoids and even ovals. Possibly more likely to be used to cut crystal. Still with the center slit and the diamonds, however.

"Everything going all right?" asks George Hurst. He is a short brisk man in his fifties, with sandy hair, a pleasant smile and the easygoing friendliness of a man who spends most of his working day being the most wide-awake and sober person in the room. I ask if it is always like this.

"Oh, this is quiet. Because of the rain. Still, we had four hundred people between eleven and two—pretty good for a hundred-seat restaurant. This place is tremendous. I was in business myself before I came here, and I worked long hours, did all the things you're supposed to and got squeezed out because of high rents. Here, nobody works long hours. Nobody runs or even walks fast. And everybody who works here is happy with their job. I guess you know that, if you've talked to other people. And so I won't bother to tell you all the same things. But you won't find anybody—anybody—who has a bad word to say about old Mr. Kubach.

"You know he pays good—even the dishwasher, because he say the dishwasher has to pay the same thing we do for a pair of shoes. And he treats everybody right—a week's pay bonus at Christmas. Holidays, he makes sure all the waitresses have corsages. For Betty Baillie's birthday he got a special pair of gold earrings the shape of the Melrose clock made up to give her. The managers go out for a Christmas party every year at the country club—a big spread, all you can drink, take the family, all on the Kubachs. You know he has never counted his money?"

I nod, delighted to hear all those good-natured sayings all over again. I am about to ask about the apple pie, when George goes on.

"You may know about it, because you hear people say it. But everybody here knows about it—and they are the ones who hand him the money. Think about that. That man trusts people. And he tells them that he trusts them. That's like telling somebody you'll pick up the tab for dinner—before they order. And for Mr. Kubach, it works. You can't argue with success. He pays a good buck. He gets a good day's work—and more. I don't want you writing this down, but he's a wonderful man."

All the groups coming in now are odd-numbered and there are never half as many women as there are men. Some of the girls have tattoos—tiny snakes or twining roses, it is impossible to tell which, down in the cleavage under the bra. A woman with a crew cut, a slither dress, and a long-haired blonde girl friend on her arm who keeps flinging the hair over her shoulders with her fingers. Out through the windows you can see the street turn blue and the street lights fade. One large guy in a T-shirt that he seems poured into has a head that is almost completely shaved except for a V of bristly hair that extends back from the front of his forehead. He is extraordinarily muscled. He walks back and forth to the men's room twelve times in an hour and is organizing some kind of temporary trade.

"He wants the *cars?*" says Jeanne with an *e*.

"Look," says a guy with a baseball player cast in gold on a chain around his neck. "They're only going to be gone a little while, I'm telling you. It's better this way. They'll take him home. Let him have the cars and don't let it get any worse."

It does not get any worse. But the group of people who have given up their cars dawdle around in a corner booth over yet another breakfast, yawn and smile and shrug, as suddenly . . . it's dawn.

Half the people with Teamster jackets and crew cuts really are Teamsters now—and they look back at the other people in Teamster jackets without recognition, but with quiet intelligence. Each realizes the other is not wearing the right uniform. But they look exactly alike—except that the real truck drivers have pencils behind their ears.

"In the pouring rain," says one of the mournful guys with no sideburns and no car either.

"It's very strange," sings Jeanne with an *e*. "Hey, look! Hey, look! The cars are coming back!"

Two silver Mercedes pull up to the door, and everybody rushes through the check-out line to pile into them.

"Hey, do something like a poem to say goodbye," says Jeanne with an *e*.

"I already have the Beatles," I say.

"No, something good—say goodbye like a writer. A writer as good as the Melrose."

The Melrose is suddenly, for the moment, almost empty.

"You get out," I say laughing. "The other one too."

"Please," says the redhead. "Do Hemingway—you know, *Farewell to Arms*."

Anything for her:

"But after I had got them out and shut the door it wasn't any good. It was like saying goodbye to a statue. After a while I went out and left the Melrose and walked back to the hotel in the pouring rain."

THREE

MARIO MAKES THE DOUGH

"My brother Mario makes the dough," says Bob D'Adamo. "He'll be in about ten-thirty, eleven. He's in law school and we let him get a late start mornings."

Bob is already at work, boning out a leg of veal—actually something closer to a whole side of veal: breast and leg and neck and a dark brown kidney cased in fat. We stand in the kitchen of Marra's, a medium-priced Italian restaurant in Philadelphia famous for its pizza.

"This is nature veal, the best, from the best supplier in town, Geurera. He'd bone it out for us. But then you don't get the bones—which I make into the veal stock. Or we might not get all the fat with the kidney, which we give to Signorina, our cleaning lady, who comes from Argentina and who wants all of it."

He puts the fat and the kidney carefully on a brown paper and wraps it.

"Enjoy," he says. "The veal stock—our veal stock—is what makes the dish. I cook the bones three or four days, depending on the weather. Summers I try to start it Mondays because we're closed Monday and it really heats up the kitchen." He pointed to an old Vulcan flattop stove, its top bellied like a bowl, clean but fire-streaked. "There's been a lot of gravy cooked on that stove. And a lot of veal stock. For almost fifty years. So this year, we're finally remodeling the kitchen—all new stoves. Which should be cooler. But I don't know—maybe we'll miss the old stuff. That's what my grandfather says, and I'll tell you, on cold winter mornings, the first thing we come in, everybody's saying, 'Hey, Bob, start up the veal stock.'

"I started back when I was twelve, helping my father in the kitchen with the cooks. I just . . . liked it. My father is the real pro. Cooks from here went to all the big Italian restaurants in the city—he taught them all, worked with them all. He runs the place now, right, Dad?"

Mario D'Adamo smiles quietly and goes on with his work, breading oysters. A short man who still has all his black hair, grown a little gray around the sideburns. In the three days I hang out in Marra's kitchen, he never raises his voice, rarely says more than a sentence at a time, seems to agree to what his sons say with a shrug or a word—and obviously runs the place.

The only other person in the kitchen now is Frankie, still in his teens, a cousin of the D'Adamos', the kind of kid who can't stand still and loves the bustle of his job. He works quietly, too, until you ask a question. Then of course he answers. Everybody calls him Chef.

"At first all I did was clean gallimar," says Bob.

He has a Philadelphia Italian accent—calamari is gallimar; manicotti is two words, manny gott; basil is Vozanagool.

"That was our business back then, bottom of the menu, gallimar, mussels, pizza and a pitcher of beer. Now we get more sophisticated customers. A bottle of wine, instead. And they want good veal. Veal *piccante*. Veal chops Marra, the top of our menu—veal chops broiled, then topped with sautéed mushrooms and peppers and onions in my veal-stock sauce—ten ninety-five—is one of our biggest sellers. Of course, a lot of people still order pizza—and split it four ways as an appetizer. We get good eaters here."

"Lots of them still save the crust and dip it in their coffee," says his father. "Or their Cokes."

"For dessert," says Bob.

"And we get a lot of people want us to wrap the crust and they take it home. They say it's for the dog. Our crust is worth eating plain, I think. I never leave any over when I have a pizza. But—enjoy. The minute you pay for it, it's yours."

"For the cheese on our pizzas we use a mixture of mozzarella, parmesan and rigott," says Bob. "It gives the pie more flavor. Lots of places just use—they call it pizza cheese, like chewing gum. It looks like milk spots all over the top and it tastes like milk to me. Cheese, if you're using real cheese, is hard to use. First of all, it changes. We get two kinds of mozzarella—Maggio and one from a little grocery store in the neighborhood where the guy makes his own mozzarella. That mozzarella is like . . . wine. Chef, grind up the cheese so you can show him how."

Frankie pulls boxes of cheese out of a big walk-in refrigerator. The commercial mozzarella is yellow-white and neatly packed in arm-long bricks. The homemade mozzarella wobbles and waves a little; it is dark golden-orange, and it does have a dark winy taste. We stand eating chunks of it as Frankie feeds it into a big Hobart grinder—mixing both mozzarellas together so that they come out like hamburger—in thin, ropy strings particolored orange and white.

"We go through cheese like . . . like a firehouse goes through water," says Frankie. "And you can quote me."

"Tell him what you always say," says Bob. "A cook works . . ."

"A cooks works from sun to sun, a chef's work is never done. And you can quote me again," says Frankie. "This mozzarella is like our secret weapon—this guy don't sell it to everybody."

"Just a corner grocery," says Bob. "He does his neighborhood business and he makes some for us. Just the guy and his father, so they can't go into big production, and we get— how much we get from them, Dad?"

His father smiles and shrugs, "Much as we can."

"We mix this two-to-one, Maggio and homemade," says Frankie. "Then I break down the grinder and we do the tomatoes. You got to have fresh tomatoes in your pizza—and you can quote me—because all canned makes it too thick. And you can't have only fresh tomatoes because that makes it too thin and watery. So we mix that half and half. We get overripes—tomatoes just about to go—because the green and the hard don't cook fast enough. You'd think overripes is cheaper because they got to sell them, right? No. They cost just as much in summer, and in winter they cost more. When they come from California and Florida, overripes is hard to find. Summer, fresh Jersey tomatoes . . . right, Bob?"

"Makes a helluva pizza," says Bob.

"You can quote me," says Frankie.

The overripes go through the machine and Bob takes me into the room beside the kitchen, the room with the pizza oven.

The oven is made of white firebrick, eight feet high, ten feet across, and is shaped like a big L, with the short leg pointing at the only window in the small room. In the window is a huge fan. Leading to the fan is a big sheet-metal vent which comes out of the top of the oven and has a little extra vent hanging down right over the door. The door looks like an old-fashion coal-furnace door, except that it swings in when it is pushed, like a mail slot. A bare bulb hangs over the swinging door, and next to it, in a hole in one of the firebricks is an ordinary kitchen knife stuck handle first and standing straight up.

"That's for breaking bubbles," says Bob. "And draining the pepperoni pizza. You get bubbles in the crust, and they burn if you don't punch them down with the knife. You know how sometimes in a pizza you see this big black bump out at the edge of the crust—that's a bubble and burnt tomato sauce. You don't see that here. And pepperoni—you can't use the very best pepperoni in a pizza. Because it burns. You have to use a pepperoni with a good fat content, which cooks without burning. But it makes an oily pizza—so you have to take the pizza out a second while it's cooking, put the knife on the edge, let the oil run off.

"My grandfather and grandmother, Salvatore and Chiarina Marra, started this restaurant 1925, about six, eight blocks away, in a much smaller place. 1927, they moved here, and

Marra's has been here ever since. 1957—'58, maybe—we bought the place next door and broke through. That's the kitchen now. This used to be everything, right here—ranges squeezed in over the corner—a mess. It's a lot easier now. This oven is fireclay brick, a special brick. You'll see, when we get it going, the bricks in the back start to glow. The best possible pizza, when you have lots of time—lots of heat built up, you turn off the heat, and you cook off the glow. This used to be a coal oven—we switched to oil back in the fifties."

An ordinary household oil burner is aimed through the bricks at the short end of the L, next to the window and the fan.

"When my grandparents moved," says Bob, "they had to move the oven, take it apart and then build it up again, brick by brick. A big job. And the guys that made ovens were skilled workers. We still have the bill from the bricklayer who had to come all the way down from New York—twelve dollars a day. A week's pay at least, in 1927. Plus you had to give him room and board—it was in the contract. It took three days. A lotta money . . . We have a gas oven, too."

Bob points to a small metal pizza oven in the corner of the room.

"We use it, too. For keeping the pies warm when the delivery man gets backed up. Once in a while, when we get rushed, we start the pies in here. But we'd never cook a pie in a gas oven. Now, let me explain this to you, because it's important. A gas oven has even heat all over, supposedly. But actually, the bottom gets cooked faster. Like when you cook something in your gas oven at home, you notice this sometimes. You get a pie from a gas oven, you get a pie that turns black and hard on the bottom. Some people like that. Enjoy. Some people never had any other kind of pizza. Our pizza gets cooked on tiles, and it actually fluffs up when it's cooked. The crust is lighter and doesn't turn black on the bottom. Plus we have to move our pie.

"This isn't a gas oven where you just put a pizza in and forget it. The back of this oven—the short part of the L—is the hot box. The whole thing heats up with the oil burner, heat comes in there and up the long part of the L. I start a pie in the back, I have to turn it around a couple times—you want to keep turning it toward the heat so it cooks even. Then when it's cooked in the hottest part of the oven, I bring it up front where the heat's lower and let it dry out. And cook through on the top, so you don't get a pizza all juice.

"So it takes about fifteen minutes to cook a pizza. I can do it in five if I have to, but I make sure I don't have to. You can tell a rushed pizza, though, here or in any other place—it's the kind that slides right off the dough when you lift it up to eat. So people come in here. They say, you know, we're going to build a brick oven of our own and go in competition. I say, fine. Build. Then in twenty years, when you learn how to cook in a brick oven, you'll be dangerous.

"Now come on back in the kitchen. It's time for Mario, who's always a little late when he was in school last night."

Mario is a little late and already a little tired. The two brothers both look like their father—but completely different. Bob is shorter, stocky, with light-brown hair. Mario is over six feet tall, thinner, with his father's black hair and a black moustache. They both have the same quiet, hardworking attitude that their father has—but they're completely different at work too. Bob is calm and unhurried and efficient; Mario is efficient and constantly asking himself questions as if to reassure himself that he knows the answers.

"I go to law school full time. Four nights a week. I'm in here all weekend. Days I study," says Mario. "What's the temperature? Seventy, seventy-five. Is it going to rain? Sixty percent chance. The Phillies in town? No, so we don't need as much dough. But the Sixers are playing, which means we need more dough. Nine-o'clock movie tonight—that means as soon as it goes on, people call up and order a pie delivered, you watch. More dough. What time is it? Nearly quarter of eleven. We'll get our rush seven, eight—all this stuff is important when you're making dough. We have a pizza man, the one who throws the pies. I'm the dough man. Mornings. Nights I run the oven, sometimes with Bob—mostly he's in the kitchen with the veal. Nace Danna is our pizza man. He's tough. I know if I got everything right when he likes the dough. Some days he doesn't say anything, I know it's not so good. Some days, I know he's unhappy when he says, 'You know what this is? Lawyer's dough.' Dough is hard. The flour changes. The yeast changes. The weather changes both of them. You take a hundred-pound sack of flour, it doesn't always weigh a hundred pounds—sometimes a pound or so less because it was weighed damp and dries out, sometimes a pound or so more. You can't— Mixing dough is no formula. And the dough man . . ."

"The dough man makes the pizza," says Frankie. "Me or Mario, Nace or anybody—you can quote us."

"O.K., we make the dough downstairs," says Mario. "Let's go."

"First," says Bob offering me a cup, "the drink of the house. My father started here working when he was twelve himself, running orders upstairs, because that used to be where the dining room was. Then he met my mother and married her, which is how we all got here. But I remember he said, 'You know, they always used to give us this coffee when we were working. And two or three cups, you start going faster and faster up and down those stairs . . .'—then he found out what it is, right, Dad?"

"Double espresso, double anisette," says his father with his quiet smile.

"We add anisette to our sausage when we grind it for the pizza," says Bob. "It gives it almost a sweet flavor you can taste right through all the other flavors in it. That's another one of our secrets . . ."

"He can start his own pizza parlor," says Frankie.

"If he wants to do the work—enjoy," says Bob.

"First he has to learn to make dough," says Mario, and we go down the wooden stairs to the cellar, drinking cupsful of black espresso laced with sweet anise-flavored liqueur. It does make you move faster. In one corner of the room is an old-fashion wringer-washer, without the wringer, and I ask if they launder their own linens.

"Laundry, in that?" Mario laughs. "That's where Uncle John

cleans the mussels. We buy used machines—you know they're hard to get now, too? And we burn them out in three or four months or so. You have to soak the mussels first in pails, then dump them in the machine, load it with water and just turn it on. We lose a few mussels—they break up in the machine. Then we have to take them out, put them in pails, give them a final scrub and take the beards off. We have clean mussels. We always did, even before the machines—but your hands used to swell up scrubbing those things. Turn red and just puff right up. Mussels change too, you know? Winter, when they get them out of cold water—they don't open up when you cook them sometimes. The mussel's good, the mussel's done—but it's closed tight.

"O.K. We're making dough. It goes into this big mixing machine here."

Mario shows me a big iron machine, painted white, something like a junior-sized cement mixer. A big flywheel on the side, a big round bin in the middle that opens all along its four-foot length and big iron blades that turn inside.

"This is an old machine. My grandfather says old is best—he bought it in 1925 when he started. And he bought it used. I don't know how old it is. It looks old."

It looks like a machine you might see in an illustration from a turn of the century magazine, all cast iron and built for the ages.

"We keep a pair of ear muffs down here—the same kind you wear on a pistol range—because the thing's so loud," says Mario. "Once it gets going, it clanks and it really almost screams. Now the first thing I got to do is get the yeast in water. And I got to use the right amount of yeast. Too much and the dough overproofs—it gets soft and sticky and . . . Nace calls it lawyer's dough. Not enough yeast, the dough won't rise, it gets hard, like plastic, you have to fight it to get it into a pie shell . . . lawyer's dough again. And the thing is, no matter how I make it, it'll keep changing. We put it in the refrigerator after we get it formed into balls, to slow it down, but it keeps right on proofing. It's growing. So what I have to do is judge, based on when our rush is going to be, what kind of weather we're having—the warmer the faster it proofs—whether it's going to rain, because the flour is heavier then and you need more yeast . . . it's touchy. This part is touchy."

Mario fills a pail with water from a hose and stands over the pail with a two-pound box of yeast, shaking it in liberally as he talks. He stops. Looks at his watch. More yeast. "Frankie, you're sure the radio said it's going to rain." That's not a question—more yeast. "We got a late start." More yeast. "Seventy degrees." A little more yeast, stopped suddenly with a little scooping motion of the box.

"Some people put sugar in—it helps the yeast work. Maybe you could use less yeast, I don't know. We never did. We never will—because we never did, really, is the reason. But I can't imagine sugar in a pizza. We add salt. Salt retards the yeast." He sprinkles from a box. "Of course, I have to figure all over again how much salt to add . . . Now." He throws a bucket of ice cubes into the mixer, then adds the bucket of yeasty water.

"I add just enough ice, which also retards the yeast . . . It's around seventy now, and the water is around the same temperature, actually the yeast works fastest between ninety and a hundred and ten . . . Now, Chef is bringing the flour"—two hundred-pound sacks from the back room—"I have to add this flour slowly . . ." He throws in flour in huge scoopfuls, five or so pounds at a time. "You can't just dump flour in. Flour is alive, too. Everything changing, everything complicated . . ."

Mario turns on the huge machine, it groans into motion, a motion it's been making once a day every day but Monday, since the beginning of this century; like all old machines it seems more animal than mechanical, as if it knew what it had to do and was eager to do it but hated to be bothered. "I gotta bad back, lifting these sacks actually, so I don't do it anymore."

Frankie rips open the top of a hundred-pound sack and lifts it from the bottom, getting it positioned so that it is across his back, open end pointed backward at the clanking machine.

"O.K.," says Mario, and Frankie lifts his back a little, dumping in flour. "O.K." Frankie stops, and Mario mixes. "O.K." Frankie straightens more.

It takes maybe a minute before Frankie stands straight up, holding the bottom of the sack in his hands, arms straight up in the air, the hundred pounds cascading into the machine. They start on the second sack and it goes the same way— Mario constantly pulling out mixes of the dough, tasting, testing, stretching it with his fingers.

"Heavy flour," he says, almost the last words I hear. The machine clangs and clongs and shudders. Mario has a knife now and motions to me with the earphones. I shake my head. "If you did this every day . . ." he says, and puts on the earphones.

The flour mix is now turning through and over the blades of the machine, and each time the blades pass, Mario cuts between them with his knife, opening a big ragged tear all along the fat white surface of the dough. The machine is making a heavy beating thumping noise. We can hear each other in the pauses between the thumps.

"Let air," Mario says.

"In," says Frankie and mouths, "You can quote me."

Air in the dough, I learn later, helps the yeast work in the dough. Mario uses two arms now, slicing with his right hand, pushing the dough back over the blades with his whole left forearm.

"Hafta watch," says Mario.

"Catch your hand," says Frankie.

"One dough man," says Mario.

"Before Mario," says Frankie.

"Thumb!" Mario mimes catching his thumb in the big, clumsy, turning blade.

"Broke."

"Terrible," I say.

"Not so," says Frankie.

"Didn't bleed," says Mario.

"We saved the dough," says Frankie. It's a family joke.

"This is touchy now," says Mario. "Don't want to get it too dry. More you mix. Dryer. It gets."

He keeps pulling bits of dough, checking the stickiness on his fingers. Tasting. Frankie tastes. Mario cuts again.

"Look at. The air holes." Big holes, like the holes in Swiss cheese, only not round, appearing in the slices when Mario cuts through with his knife. "It's proofing. Fast." Another slice. "Look at. White lumps. Of flour." White flecks, the size of the holes, are spread through the dough. "That's. What. You want."

He grabs a handful. The thumping is faster now, and we don't even try to talk over. Mario just tastes, knifes and tastes, hands to Frankie who tastes. Finally he tastes and takes again and tastes, and hands a lump to Frankie with a look that is not a question. Frankie nods. Mario pulls the white handle of the machine. The silence is sudden.

"We figure on having an early rush so I made it a little dry, if this was a late night—Saturday, I'd make it not so dry, and it'd dry itself out. Chef, get Bob down here to help roll, this is proofing fast. You're sure the temperature is seventy? It's really proofing."

He knifes out a huge chunk of dough and takes it to a stainless-steel restaurant table, six feet long. On the table he puts an antique balance scale. "This is at least as old as the dough machine. Maybe older." It works by moving a hanging weight along an arm and then loading the dough on a flat metal disk, which has worn itself to a low lustrous shine from years of use.

"My father does this automatically," says Mario. "We use one pound eight and a half ounces of dough for a large pizza, half that for a small—twelve and a quarter ounces."

He takes a dough cutter—a wooden handle worn almost to the color of skin and as smooth as skin, with a metal blade with the same luster as the scale disk—and begins cutting chunks from the ragged pile of dough on the table. Frankie is back down again, with Anthony, a brother-in-law of Mario's, who also works in the kitchen. Mario cuts dough, weighs, cuts off a bit if the dough is too heavy, adds a bit if it's light. When there are about ten chunks he stops and gives the knife to Frankie. "Frankie's better at judging," he says.

"A chef's work . . ." says Frankie, and begins cutting.

Mario and Anthony begin by punching the dough down with their hands, then kneading it quickly in a folding motion. After the first one or two, they are kneading two-handed, two lumps at a time. Their wrists bend almost as far forward and backward as possible in a single fluid motion. The ragged lumps turn into neat round domes.

"Fucking wrists," says Mario.

"Fucking arms," says Anthony. I can see the muscles in their forearms flex and relax, flex and relax.

Mario Senior quietly comes down the stairs and takes over the blade. Frankie has kept up with two kneaders, each working on two rolls at once. He switches to kneading the dough. Mario Senior is, without seeming to hurry or strain, turning out lumps of dough faster than all three can knead. From time to time, he stops cutting and kneads himself—with shorter, but not noticeably quicker, motions with his wrists. But he is the fastest at kneading, too. Sweat on all the brows.

"This is proofing fast. Coming up good, you think, Dad?"

"Looks good," says his father. "Very fast."

"Chef, get the mussels out now," says Mario. "Uncle John won't have to open the refrigerator door and cool it off, this is very fast proofing. Check the temperature, it should be no more than thirty. You know," Mario says to me, "veal is easy, you buy the best, you cut it the way you want it, you put it in the refrigerator, nothing happens to it. Dough—keeps right on proofing. If we don't get this in the box fast it'll be all overproofed and flabby . . . lawyer's dough."

Everybody works. Frankie goes back and cuts out another armload of dough from the machine. Another load.

"Three hundred large you think, Dad?"

His father shrugs and nods.

"Two hundred small?"

"About."

"Hundred and fifty?"

"Yeah . . . sounds good."

"You know, this is hard work," says Mario with a hard-working smile. "We got forearms like rocks, all of us. And it used to be easier—tell him, Dad."

The father smiles.

"We had a wood table, a wood table we had for fifty years," says Mario, "and they made us switch to stainless steel, the Board of Health. Wood is a lot easier, there's more resistance, more friction, it does part of the work for you. Stainless steel is slippery, you're chasing the dough half the time . . . They said they were afraid of splinters. Fifty years we had the same wood table, and we never had splinter one. We never got splinters, we never saw splinters in the dough, we never had a customer say anything about splinters. And if you saw how smooth and white that table was—well, that's why a lot of people voted for Reagan, to get the government out of business . . . Am I right, Dad?"

The father smiles. Maybe there is a political difference in the D'Adamo family; but I don't know, I never asked.

The dough is laid in plastic trays that stack up four or five feet high before Frankie pulls them away and gets them into the big walk-in refrigerator. The kneading takes ten or fifteen minutes—and exhausts all the kneaders. The temperature of the room, from the dough and the yeast and the work, keeps going up. On this cool early spring day, I am sweating too, just standing there watching when the last tray is carried off.

"Now . . ." says the father, in the single sentence he says that is not in answer to a question, "we have one more thing to do. All go upstairs and take a break."

We take a break. Bob has been baking lasagna in the pizza oven, and makes a calzone for lunch—a pizza shell folded over a mix of ricotta and prosciutto and baked.

"Calzone is really just baked ravioli, that's what my grandmother used to call it," says Bob. "You know, she's been dead fifteen years and people still come in and say, 'Where's the big woman who make the pizza?' She would make us calzone for lunch when we came down the restaurant . . . us kids would go crazy when we saw that, huh, Mario? I try, I still can't get it as even brown as she did . . ."

It is superb calzone.

Uncle John cleans the mussels. The restaurant takes its slow rest before dinner.

Nace Danna, the pieman, has his apron on, and the first couple orders—green for restaurant, pink for takeout—up on clips over his head before I realize he's there. Frankie has brought up the first four or five trays of dough. Nace lifts out the white dome, shiny slick now and swelled up half again as large.

"Hey!" he says, calling into the kitchen. "Where's Mario? Mario in today? Mario . . . this dough"—Nace has one of those drawling, slow ways of talking that make everything sound sarcastic, even when it's not—"this dough . . . it's Beauty Full."

Nace takes a lump, puts it in a floured, stainless-steel bowl, dumps flour on the marble counter in front of him, throws the dough ball, flattens it, then takes the sheet of dough and passes it back and forth between his forearms three or four times. One toss in the air. Then he catches it on his forearms again, puts it on a wooden paddle about three feet long. Looks up at the orders, reaches for the bowl of fresh tomato and canned tomato mix, scoops some over the dough, adds some cheese, half pepperoni, half sausage. He turns and knocks the door of the brick oven so it flaps in, gives the paddle a shake, and the pizza scoots off and into the oven.

I finally get to ask somebody why piemen throw pizzas in the air.

"It evens the dough, so does passing it over your arms," he says. "Here I also have to make a lip, an edge around the pie. We make a wet pie, because we dry it out in the oven while it cooks. No lip—and the sauce would shoot right off the pie when I get it in the oven. Christ"—he is genuinely delighted—"this is Beauty Full Dough, Mario. I could make a thousand pies with dough like this. Bad dough—you know when you get bad dough that the dough man is important—you have to work so much harder. You throw it on your arms, it sticks, it's heavy, it won't spread. Your arms get tired fighting dough. I'm in my forties now, so I been doing this twenty-five years . . . I stopped a couple times, had jobs, had a place of my own . . . I always come back to pies. I like it. Like tonight, with dough like this—I love it."

Mario is at the door of the oven. He has to bend almost double to look in. He takes a long wooden pole, eight feet long, with a metal disc, around a foot across, on the end. He lifts the pie. Gives it a turn and pushes it all the way to the back of the oven. Each pie is moved four or five times, turned each time so that a new side is toward the flame, moved steadily toward the front where Mario punches down the bubbles, tilts it slightly on the pepperoni side to let oil run off into a plastic bag at his feet and moves it to the coolest side of the oven where it will dry for five minutes. Within minutes, there are eight pies in the oven, and Mario is bent over into his permanent crouch of the night.

"This oven"—he straightens up after a few hours, stretching out and bending backward—"was made for midgets. My hardest job is bending over. We have to clean this every couple years. Usually for spills and sauce drips and stuff, I just sprinkle in salt and it burns right off. Just a little smoke." He demonstrates. "You see what salt does to grease on tiles, you believe it when doctors tell you it's bad for you. Imagine what it does to your insides. We cleaned this last year . . . These bricks hold heat. The floor of the oven is sand, over that, interlocking tiles, and the tiles buckle—not buckle, just bump up out of their lock with the heat. After years of that it gets wavy in there and we have to take out the tiles, smooth the sand, lock them all back down again. So we turn off the oil burner. Close for a week. Three days, you still can't do anything. Finally we take ice, dump in ice, squirt it with CO_2 fire extinguishers that drop the temperature, get out the tiles, smooth the sand—and have to work on the roof of the oven. You have to lay down in there to do that. We load the floor with pizza boxes, the bags that the mussels come in, it's the middle of winter, no heat in the whole place, and you lay in there an hour you're burning your back. We had Senator Heinz come to visit us, and he saw the oil burner, he says, turn it off, conserve energy. We turned it off for him and cooked off the glow—but we never leave the burner on all night, we switch it on, switch it off, we're always cooking partly off retained heat. This oven saves energy."

Bob and Mario Senior spell Mario at the oven from time to time, so he can straighten up, walk around sit down for a drink of the house. There is a glass sheet between Nace and the waitresses, with a hole in the middle for talking through and a slot at the bottom for passing the pies—something like the teller's glass in an old-fashion bank. I ask if that's because of the Board of Health, too.

"No," says Bob. "We got the bowls of food up there and guys'll come up and order a pizza-to-go themselves—they keep sticking their fingers in the bowls, pulling out pepperoni, sausage, mushrooms . . . right, Dad?"

"I don't grudge," says the father quietly.

"Right, but . . ."

"Ask me and I'll give you some. But we can't have people's hands in the food."

"Louise dropped a pie down the dumbwaiter," says Frankie from the next room. "Small, all cheese."

Nace makes up a new one quickly. It goes in the oven, then is spun quickly to the back. "Five minutes," says Bob. "If they're in a hurry, try to hold them off."

"A large pie. Pepperoni and sausage. Extra cheese. Down the dumbwaiter," says Frankie.

"Hey, which is it?" says Nace. "Large or small?"

"Which would it be, in the middle of the rush?" says Bob.

"Both," says the father. And both pies are quickly made up.

Mario is back, bending into his work.

"No oil tonight," says Nace.

"Mozzarella is funny, too," says Mario. He turns and spins three different pies, moving them forward. "Come look at the oven."

I look in—the whole back wall looks like the dull red glow under white ash—like charcoal when it's perfect for barbecuing. Mario switches off the oil burner, cooking off the glow, and stands up to tell me about mozzarella.

"It's made from milk. Milk is different. Sometimes, in the spring especially, there's a lot of shallots in the grass. The cows eat the shallots and it affects the milk. I don't know why, but the cheese is drier. We have a bottle of olive oil by the pieman so if he sees the cheese is dry he can add a little on the top . . . Sometimes, the mozzarella is selling fast—lots of pizzas being made, lots of customers, and Maggio or our corner store can't hold it back to age it. So we have to dry it out—instead of putting it in the refrigerator for the day, we put it down by the oven for a couple hours, so it cooks or melts but it loses some water. Now, you see we keep our tomatoes—they're ground and mixed—in a covered pot, because we can't refrigerate them. If the tomatoes are cold, they won't let the cheese melt right. But we can't let the cheese get too warm or it gets gummy and sticks together and Nace can't sprinkle it easy . . ."

"Look at him write," laughs Nace. "Let me ask you something—did you ever think before that making a pizza was so complicated?"

"It doesn't have to be complicated, Nace," says Mario. "There's places that buy their dough, ready made up, kneaded, cooled, just stick it in the refrigerator—always made the same, same formula, frozen maybe . . . simple."

"Yeah," laughs Nace. "Simple . . . crap. That dough, I made pies with it. Like leather, pulling at it, or like taffy it's so sticky. It won't brown—comes out of the oven as white as it went in on top, all burnt black under. Feels like a wet blanket on your arms. It makes you hate to go to work. Now this dough"—he gives it three or four fast swipes over his forearms and tosses it spinning into the air—"this dough is Beauty Full."

FOUR

MAD AS A BATTER

THE PROBLEM IS

"I've made a new discovery," says Harry Kulkowitz, philosopher and restaurateur. "People who complain about slow service are people who are not very compatible among themselves. Think about it for a minute. If you're with somebody you like in a restaurant, you sit at the table, have a little wine, a little conversation. Look in each other's eyes. If you're bored by the person you're with, you start looking around for the waitstaff and taking your boredom out on them. So, since we will never be a fast-food restaurant—because we cook everything to order—the problem is not slowness. We're *famous* for slowness. The problem is—how can we attract more lovers to our restaurant."

Harry Kulkowitz is a restaurant lover. He is co-owner—with his great and good friend Vickie Seitchik—of the Mad Batter, a very successful Cape May, New Jersey, restaurant. The Batter has been in business for six years now and has survived all the usual restaurant crises. The week when the staff had to be told there was no money for a payroll and they'd have to work on trust; the silent partner who got so noisy he had to be bought out; the dishwasher who quit in the middle of the dinner rush . . .

"But that happens every year," says Harry. "I wish I had a nickel for every dish I washed. Getting a good dishwasher is almost impossible. Keeping a good dishwasher . . . We're living in a new world, with a new type of person. This generation does not care about security—you can't bribe them with money. That has its advantages in a restaurant like this. We don't want robots—because a restaurant is not a machine. But dishwashers . . . One summer, I never had so much trouble with dishwasher quitting—and I complained to a friend of mine who operates another restaurant. He was having the same trouble—with the *same* dishwashers. We checked with other owners. We finally figured it out. A bunch of dishwashers had decided among themselves to have a contest—how many restaurants could they quit on in a single season. They were going from place to place, driving us all crazy. How many times have you ever read about a problem like that—in all those articles about starting restaurants, nobody ever talks about dishwashers. I thought I finally solved it—I paid Mac four seventy-five an hour. He deserves more—dishwashing is important—but that's all I could afford. Still, I told him I'd give him a bonus of twenty-five cents an hour for every hour that he worked if he'd stay the whole season with me. August comes. It's hot, it's a weekend, we're crowded—and we can't serve the customers because we have no clean plates. And no dishwasher, because he's late. He comes in, I start to yell—just start to yell—and he quits. He was going to give up all that money—twenty-five cents an hour for four months—just because I got mad. What did I do? I stopped everything, I sat down, I talked him out of it. I just couldn't face doing all those dishes again. The first thing a restaurant owner has to learn to do is, learn how to get along with his dishwasher."

Harry's problem is nothing like Tell Erhardt's or Richard Kubach's. Harry is not a trained chef, running his restaurant from the kitchen. He does not have a permanent staff of older workers—he has to staff his restaurant all over again every year, and he deals mostly with the new young restaurant worker, a worker who is not at all interested in security (like workers at the Melrose) and who is not European trained (like most of the workers at Erhardt's). Harry does not improve his restaurant by shopping around at big distribution centers—he very deliberately does all his buying from local suppliers. That's good business for him, because it's good public relations with the small but important population of Cape May that lives in the city year round. Harry cannot even improve his restaurant too fast.

"We just got better bread," he says. "For years, I've been complaining about the local bread—outside of the big cities where you can still find ethnic bakeries of French bread, American bread is all just one variation or another—soft and springy and airy and tasteless. I found a new local bakery that makes better bread. So I got it. And so I made a new enemy. My old bread supplier not only hates me for switching my business, he hates me for liking the new bread. 'Taste it and then taste mine,' he tells me angrily. 'See how hard the new stuff is? How nice and soft mine is? And it'll keep for a week without going stale. Heat it over and over again and mine doesn't get hard.' I can't just tell him that his bread is lousy, so I have to answer him nice. But I have to be firm. This new bread is much better. And since it's local, I have to buy it. I buy the very best from my local people that I can get. Part of my job is educating them, in a nice way, about what the best means. Bread is one of the places where I haven't done that job right—but it's getting better, anyway. At last."

"And remember, every year I am a new restaurant owner. The Batter closes down for five months a year. Each time we open, it's like opening up all over again. Some old people, some new people. I have one member of my staff who quit or was fired every year for the past four years. I hire him back. Because—and you can write this down—if you're above six on the Kulkowitz scale, I put up with anything. The Kulkowitz scale is skill and creativity—from one to ten. This person is an eight or nine and I am always sure we're going to work things out. This year I need a new breakfast chef, and a woman came in, Virginia Budd-Packer. She's been a professional actress, she's a graduate in a holistic healing, she's never had any experience as a chef. But talking to her, I could feel that she understood what's important about this place. You know, we waste a lot of food. I encourage the staff to do that—I don't want food going out of the kitchen that isn't right. I'd rather have the cook tell the waitperson, 'I messed up,' and throw away bad food. Then the waitperson tells the customer. Remember—this is important, too; if you want to start a restaurant, don't start lying to your customers. If the food is going to take a while, tell them; if the chef has to start all over, tell them that too. It's the waitperson who tells the customer it's going to take five minutes when it's going to take ten that gets you in trouble. Virginia understands that. She looks at the plates going out of the kitchen, and she stops anything that looks wrong. That's important. Because my job isn't in the kitchen—my job is out on the floor. Because a restaurant is not just food—not even just good food—every restaurant needs a personality. A presence. A human being to relate to. That's my job. And the problem is—getting me out of the kitchen."

I followed Harry Kulkowitz for a week in late spring as he reopened his restaurant. He never quite succeeded in getting out of the kitchen—partly, I think, because he likes the heat. He did tell me more about restaurants than I thought there was to know; and I discover that the problem is—I spent so much time taking notes on what he said, that I've never thought about describing the person, the human being. Harry is not easy to describe. He has gray-white hair and a gray-white Vandyke; he is about five feet five or six, thin—and full of nervous energy. And relaxed. He is so calm about his restlessness, and so reasonable about his perfectly unreasonable demands for perfection, that he is able to get everybody on his side. He wanders from dining room to kitchen, to refrigerator, to the new construction that will turn his big backyard into a patio. He is constantly talking, discussing, cajoling, thinking—improving, improving. Leaving little notes on the bulletin board:

> WAITSTAFF: Please do not use sugar packets to prop up short legs on tables. A folded piece of cardboard works just as well, is cheaper and does not leak sugar underfoot by the end of the night.

"No detail is too small," says Harry. "Right now, we're working on improving toast. And butter. Breakfast is a very important meal at the Batter. Our omelets are among our most popular items. But we put the toast on the same plate as the omelet. I was traveling around this winter, eating at restaurants, thinking of improvements—when I realized, if you put jelly on your toast, you don't have anywhere to put it except back down on the plate—which is all full of mushroom or cheese omelet. So I want us to have separate plates from toast. The waitstaff says it's too many plates and they don't fit on the trays. I thought of getting bigger trays—but the waitstaff says that the plates won't all fit on the table. I tried it. It *is* too many plates for a small table. We have to think about this.

"Butter. For dinner we have butter pats wrapped in foil. Expensive, but it cuts down on waste. For breakfast we have butter on tiny squares of cardboard, with a sheet of tissue on top. It's cheaper, and it's perfectly good enough for pancakes. But the waitstaff is careless with this butter. We have it sitting in a tray at the kitchen pickup and they simply grab—they knock off some of the papers, they squeeze them together. In their hurry—and I tell them not to hurry—they waste a lot of butter, by making it too ugly to serve to the customer. So I moved the butter to the refrigerator. They should be able to stop one second on the way out, stoop down, balance the tray, and get the butter out of the half refrigerator we have for cream and butter. But—nobody admits it—*but* the dinner butter is showing up on the breakfast table. Possibly it's just carelessness. Possibly it is the waitstaff's way of demonstrating that they just don't like the new system. I could move the dinner butter to the big refrigerators for the breakfast hours. But that might not be the problem. The problem is—you have to figure out what the real problem is."

LIKE A GALLERY OF ART

"I ran an art gallery before I ran a restaurant," says Harry. "But, of course, I did a lot of things. I was a soldier in the Second World War. I was a radio operator, a photographer—I was the only Jewish marble and tile setter in New York until I quit. Because of the fights. You know, marble and tile setters in those days were all either Irish or Italian, and we'd get along fine. But the bosses were different. One time in Brooklyn we're working for a general contract putting marble cornices on a building. A piece falls off and hits a woman on the arm—because they hadn't taken proper safety precautions: so we had to stop until they set them up. The general contractor climbs up a ladder—from just a floor below—and asks us why we're sitting around. I tell him that the woman hit in the arm had complained. He says, 'Oh, those Heebs—always complaining.' I kicked him off the ladder. Actually I just put my foot against the ladder and pushed the ladder off the roof. He was only shaken up . . .

"But I wanted to tell you about my gallery in Philadelphia. I sold it in 1975 and retired. It was a good gallery, but I just couldn't go on and keep up with the pressures to stay in business—which is the pressure to do shows I didn't like.

That got more and more difficult. The rent got higher and higher. And—this might sound dramatic and corny, but it's true—I work with too much intensity to bother with things I don't believe in. I come from a working-class family—in the Bronx, New York—and I know what it is when people are cheated by somebody who probably just needs to pay the rent. So I got out of it and came down here to Cape May. I knew some people down here who were interested in the arts—I'm a photographer, and I started teaching photography classes. But Vickie—Vickie is the practical person of the family and knows me better than I know myself—Vickie just said, 'This is ridiculous. You can't retire. You'll drive both of us crazy.' I was bored to death. So I looked around for a business to go in—and the one thing Cape May needed was a good restaurant.

"Now, this is interesting—that was the one thing Cape May didn't need, in 1946, or '56, or '66. But sometime in the 1970s restaurants went from being these dreary places you had to eat in when you stayed at a hotel to cultural centers almost. Like a gallery of art. This generation wants more than anything else to be satisfied with their work—they want fulfillment. They don't want a safe life, they want a good day. That's the kind of attitude that makes this restaurant possible. You know, we had a young woman in here once who was trained in a big hotel. She could turn out sauces like a machine, she could turn out dishes like a conveyor belt . . . And I fired her. She was computerizing us, making all these mechanical sauces in advance, as if the idea was serve a thousand people in an hour. Our biggest reputation is—we're slow. I felt bad about firing her, but she said she wouldn't be out of a job long. And she wasn't—I think she wound up at Stouffer's.

"Anyway, Vickie said to start a business, and I decided to start a restaurant. So we looked around and found this place. The Carroll Villa—which is why it's called the Mad Batter—a rundown old rooming house with a big dark dining room and a big bare porch. The problem was—nobody wanted to eat in the dining room it was so dark; and you couldn't eat on the porch because the sun in the summer is too hot, and it drives people crazy to eat and sweat at the same time. So this place was cheap. The owners couldn't put up awnings because Cape May is on the Historical Register, and you can't change the appearance of any building in that case. We almost didn't get it—but we did a little research. And we were able to find a picture of this place with awnings. That saved it for us. I was teaching photography at the time and I had this student, Dennis Finley—my best student. The two of us had a rapport. When Dennis said he could do something, you knew he could do it. He's gone on now, to professional photography. He's very good, very high quality. Dennis said, 'I can cook. Breakfast.' 'Fine,' I said. 'You be the cook and I'll be the waiter.' And we got together twelve thousand dollars and got an option to buy the Villa—because I didn't want to have the problems of rent I had with my gallery. And we set to work, cleaning up, painting, getting awnings—that was my biggest original investment, thirty-five hundred dollars, I think—and I started scrounging up kitchen equipment, because the stuff that was here was really unusable. We got the tables, which get wobbly, and the antique cane chairs—which cost forty dollars each to recane and always wear out—I got a storeroom full of chairs that need caning. And then, a week before we opened, Vickie, who is a practical person, mentioned that we had never tasted anything that Dennis cooked. Well, that was a detail I had overlooked, so I had him cook us a breakfast—and, as I never tire of reminding Vickie, it was delicious. When I know I can trust somebody, they can always be trusted.

"At first we were only open for breakfast—but it turns out that Vickie had a friend who had a friend who was working as a prep person, making salads and cooking vegetables, at the Fish Market, a very good Philadelphia restaurant. This was Susan Trilling, and she showed up here one day with a whole lot of food—in a shoe box. She'd cooked it in Philadelphia and brought it down on the bus for us to taste. We hired her. We started out gathering a staff the same way I gathered artists for my gallery. We traveled around—we heard people were bored with their jobs. We interviewed. We looked for the kind of person we wanted—you know we didn't want easy people to get along with necessarily. We didn't want ordinary workers who would get content—the fire goes out and the quality goes down. There's not a year that goes by I don't say to myself I'm quitting this business. But I won't. I know I'd rather die this way than any other. This restaurant is a very real part of my life. And it's not like the gallery. I don't have to make any compromises on quality. I know that everybody who buys something here is getting good value, something real.

"Of course we had problems. Vickie cut out this little list from a business magazine for me—'Why Businesses Go Under.' From one to ten. One, going into business with little or no experience; two, not enough capital; three, plunging in without testing the market on a small scale . . . I forget them all, but I should remember, because when Vickie handed me the list she said, 'Look, we did every one of these.' The first year, we did almost go under. I had to call the waitstaff together and tell them there was no money to pay them. They either had to work a week waiting for their checks or they had to leave."

"Harry," I finally interrupt to say, "why do you insist on calling people waitstaff and waitperson?"

"Why, I always have," says Harry. "To too many people, a waitress is just somebody you pinch on the ass—and leave a quarter tip. There's no reason that women should be treated any different—the waitperson is the one who really determines what your meal is going to be like. They bring it to you quickly, they explain the menu, they represent the restaurant. Some of the customers make fun of me—'Harry,' they say, 'will you call my waitperson?' But they treat the staff better because of it, I think. I believe.

"The first year, we had some problems with the waitstaff. We had a lot of people working here who were teachers—they're off for the summer and they thought it would be fun to work in a restaurant. It is fun—if you want to work. But teachers are very . . . vocal. And eloquent. We had a lot of complaints, a lot of meetings. One of the teachers, a very nice person, even got himself elected chairman of the meetings—and he made me raise my hand when I wanted to talk. So when I told everybody that they might not get paid at the end of the week, I also told them—if you stay, you stay because you believe in me. No more of these shitty meetings. No more raising my hand when I want to talk. It was a great crisis for the restaurant—and that very week everything turned around. We've increased business ever since. Every year our receipts are bigger than last year, bigger than inflation. We get great reviews. In *Philadelphia Magazine*. In the Washington *Post*. For the third straight year, the Atlantic City *Press* has chosen us one of the four best of the Jersey Shore . . . We're a success. And we're constantly improving. The reason is that when it comes to food, I don't dictate. I'm like a gallery director showing my artists. This is really true. The details, the details, we're always working on. But you have to assemble the best talent you can, and then trust *them* to create. So you should spend a lot of time with the staff—they make me, I don't make them. We have struggles. I know, for example, that we need a vegetarian dish on the menu—not just fish—completely vegetarian. My dinner chef, George Pechin, is no vegetarian. 'What is life without pork?' he says. He does wonderful pork dishes. But he also does a wonderful dish that is filo leaves wrapped around braised cabbage and walnuts. It tastes wonderful—but he wants to call it cabbage strudel, which doesn't sound wonderful. Food is food, he says—and he's right. But getting people to try good food is my job. We're still discussing the name of that dish. Mindy Silver is another dinner chef. George travels in the off-season. She goes down to Florida and works in another kitchen. I visited her in her winter job—a restaurant called Tuxedo—Tux—and she got me to try smoked bluefish and smoked shrimp. There's a smoker you can buy for three thousand dollars, and you can smoke things even in marinade. Chicken smoked in Grand Marnier—you've never tasted anything like it. I bought the machine. We'll have to sell a lot of fish and a lot of chicken to make back the money. But we will. I didn't come up with the recipes, though—Mindy did. The salesman brought the machine to the restaurant and started explaining it to us—and we quickly found out that he didn't know as much about the machine as Mindy did.

"That's how you make a restaurant a success—take good people and let them experiment, let them create. You have to talk to the waitstaff and kitchen staff if you want to know what makes a good restaurant. First, they know more about it than I do. And second, I have to get back in the kitchen—I think I have another idea about the toast and butter."

WAITSTAFF AND KITCHENSTAFF

"I was an art major in school," says Robin Fedderman, a tall, dark-haired and dark-eyed waitperson in her mid-twenties. "Art and special education. But I found out I couldn't do it— the same building, the same room, the same kids, day after day. It was crazy. There was only one thing you could do that was wrong—not come in on time. And I found out the only time I can get in on time is when *I* say what 'on time' is . . . I live in Cape May—my family is here—and I always was waitressing off and on through school. Last year I worked at a restaurant in a fancy hotel and made a lot of money. My mother said I should go back—but here, first of all, Harry makes sure we have the time to talk to the customers—explain the menu, ask how everything is. We want to know because he wants to know—if somebody doesn't like something, it's a major tragedy. We really care about the food here. Then if I'm on mornings, I might throw on a pair of shorts and a T-shirt, dinners I might dress up more—but there's nothing phony about the clothes we wear. I told my mother, I can dress like I want at the Batter—I'm not going back to that hotel and walk around with a doily on my head, dressed up in a black polyester tutu! I won't be a *waitress!* And I won't. I like it here. The only problem is with people who expect this to be some kind of fancier McDonald's. You have to explain to them: open your bottle of wine, sit down, take it easy, everything here is cooked to order. When you get it you'll realize: this is a better way."

"I came here to get away from the Midwest," says Daniel Peterson, a waitperson about the same age as Robin, with a neat beard that seems to fringe his face rather than grow on it. "The Midwest is the place all writers seem to want to get away from." Daniel is proofing the typescript of a thick book as we talk. "Kind of a novel, kind of autobiographical. I got started here as a dishwasher—because that's the kind of job you don't feel bad about quitting. There's no implied contract that you'll stay on till you're sixty-five—I mean, *everybody* knows about dishwashers. Waiting is the same kind of job. You're not tied down—and when you're finished, you're finished. You walk out free—nothing held over to worry about tomorrow. All the pressures are immediate pressures, and you can only work them out by working together. So restaurant work is social work—you don't find much of that in America anymore. People sit in offices at different desks, writing. They get money for it. But it's not work. It's just a job."

Claudia Gittings, a waitperson, has a degree in French Literature—and enters law school this fall. Joe Lotozo, a night *sous-chef,* started out as a teaching assistant in the Philadelphia public schools. Ellen Shaw, breakfast and dessert chef, took courses in restaurant management in business college, "But I'd been a cocktail waitress and even *I* knew that the courses didn't have anything to do with restaurants, so I quit. I started working in an Italian restaurant—the only person with an Irish name in the whole place. They called me Spud. All I did was antipasto—but the guy who made the ice cream quit and they were very proud of their homemade ice cream. So I just learned it. I came down here because I heard about the Batter, and Harry said they'd never had their own ice cream, but he'd buy a machine. We'll have ice cream, sorbets—he's getting a beautiful machine, the best there is. I might do a little fill-in breakfast cheffing, but I expect to spend the whole summer making fresh-fruit frozen desserts from blueberries and strawberries . . . It's more like play than work. Even when the pressure's on, when you're turning out breakfast orders, restaurant people love the pressure. It gets—this sounds silly—it gets in your blood. You have to have a sense of humor, you have to be able to let off steam, you have to be able to forget about it afterwards. I can't imagine doing anything else. I did have a nine-to-five job once, sitting behind a desk. I can't handle it." Ellen is poaching eggs for eggs Benedict and has just discovered that someone used the last of the hollandaise. She bends over a large bowl, whipping egg yolks and pouring in butter, glancing from time to time at the poaching eggs. Her blond hair tied back with a headband made of a twisted kerchief, yelling across the room to tell someone to ring for the waitress whose order this is, she looks as if she could handle anything. I say so.

"Well," she says, laughing, "I gave it a week. And I can *not* handle it. Two! Two! Where's waitperson number two? Here you go. English muffin. Ham. Two poached. And"—with a final shisk, triumphantly—"hollandaise! Don't forget the sprig of fresh mint to make it look pretty—you got your eggs Benedict."

The waitress picks up and leaves a bunch of orders. Ellen sticks them, in order, in a row across the big stainless-steel shelves that separate her station from the waitstaff. They hang at eye level, and she's reading as she talks to me. "What was I saying?" Two eggs slide into the big pan of boiling water for poaching, a slice of ham is sautéed in butter. "Oh, I know—I can't handle it. I can't handle those boring jobs."

100 PEOPLE TO DINNER—AND VICKIE SEITCHIK

"Tomorrow's going to be insane," says Vickie Seitchik, a small trim woman with dark hair and a very quiet air of meaning everything she says. "The Cape May County Art League is having a fund-raising dinner. One hundred people, on a Saturday night. I can't think of another restaurant that would accommodate a party of a hundred, can you? But Harry says that the fund-raiser is important, and he's right. Not just for the Batter —but because we want to be good citizens. That's an important part of running a restaurant. So not only did we give them a good price—we also let them choose among four entrees, two soups and three desserts. The chef and I decided to give them all the same salad dressing, but we haven't told Harry yet. He's the one who insisted they had to have four entrees to choose from. I hate to sound like Harry, Harry, Harry—but this really is *his* restaurant. We keep asking him to cut down the number of entrees, but somehow they just seem to grow and grow. Well, it's a challenge—like tomorrow night. We had everybody order in advance. We bought all the food. And then I thought to count and see if we had enough dishes. We didn't. So we had to run into Philadelphia and buy some salad plates and bread-and-butters—things you never think to use a hundred of at the same time. We have a system worked out—we'll do it. You'll see . . . We have a count of all the entrees— chicken, fish, spare ribs or a completely vegetarian rice and nut and vegetable salad. We'll have a countperson . . ."

It seems to me that Vickie is improvising as she talks, but on the big night, the Batter is alive with bustle, purposeful and otherwise. Outside in the dining room, the Art League has set up a bar—people are already talking in Benefit just a little louder and little more pleased with themselves than usual. In the corner called the cold station, the two sons—Harry's and

Vickie's—make the house salad in huge bowls, doling it out on seventy-six plates (all that will fit on the metal shelves). They decorate each plate with two tomato wedges and a sprinkle of parsley, trying to get all of them to look like equal portions—not an easy task with chopped romaine and cucumbers and onion. George Pechin, the head dinner chef, has already supervised the smoking of the spare ribs, a big rack for each person who ordered them.

"Then we covered them with barbecue sauce, put them in the oven—these are good ribs," he says. "What is life without pork?"

I ask George how he got to be a chef, and as he works he talks.

"I got a part-time job at an inn called Coventry Forge back in the '60s—a wonderful place; still is. We made our own mayonnaise, we made our own *crème fraîche*. We did everything ourselves. I worked with Vickie Renson, a chef who went on to buy her own restaurant in Philadelphia, and then I quit to go to school. Business administration." He laughs. "Then I wasted two years and went back to restaurants. Worked in Philadelphia for a while—but I came down here in the summer, and I liked the Batter. I like the life. I work seven months a year and then I travel. Last year, Malaysia, India, Sri Lanka. This year, Egypt. I'm only going for three months this time—my parents are getting pissed off that I'm never home for Christmas. O.K., the ribs are in the oven. Chicken paprika comes out of the oven. The sauce gets reduced on top of the stove—lots of sour cream, a good recipe. The fish is broiled bluefish—all ready for the broiler. We don't have anything but standard ranges. Wait—we have a microwave. I use it to cook through somebody's fish if they claim it's too rare. But I tell people rare fish tastes better, if they'll only try it."

George is working constantly as he talks. Slight, blond, a Southeast Asian tan that makes him two or three shades darker than anyone else, blond hair, a quiet manner. Vickie comes in to say that the Art League is sitting down. Six of the best waitstaff are gathered around.

"Only two soups; this one is easy," says George. "Where's the countperson?"

The countperson appears—a woman with an ordinary yellow pad.

"Only take five bowls on a tray," says the countperson, "so we don't lose count. Remember to look at the place cards. Everybody has a yellow block crayoned on their card if they want *crème de cresson,* blue if they want cream of mushroom. First, five *cresson."* She makes a check on the yellow pad. "Five mushroom." Another check. Each bowl gets its sprig of mint, each is inspected by the waitperson—any stray slurp from the ladle is wiped off—a quick, and careful, production line is set up.

"Too many people, Vickie says," a waitperson, who has worn her tuxedo, comes in to say. "Half bring the trays out to waitstations, half deliver the food."

Half the waitstaff disappears. I walk out to the dining room —now a babble of hungry voices—and watch how smoothly it all goes.

"Next course, salad."

Not much problem of choice here—only one of space. For the first thirty-two salads that disappear, thirty-two new salads have to be made and decorated and evened and set on trays. Nothing fancy—just fast, breathless work.

"Entrees!" says the countperson.

"O.K., guys, this is the hard part," says Robin Fedderman, waitperson without a doily or tutu. "Fast as McDonald's, *haut* as *cuisine."*

Four different color blocks on the place cards tell the waitpeople who gets what.

"So much better than that awful wineglass up for chicken and down for steak," says Robin. "Where'd we get this system?"

"Five at a time," says the countperson.

"I'm taking five," says Robin.

"And don't forget the sprig of mint."

But Robin, who has not forgotten it, is already gone.

The dinner moves quietly along at its predetermined pace—very fast for the Batter, about normal for big party dinners. Two problems—Robin comes in to announce that "we need three more ribs!"

"You can't," says George, quietly but firmly. "The counterperson counted, and they got what they ordered. Somebody's changing their minds—and they can't change it to ribs, because we don't have any more. Tell them to change it to chicken. I made some extra chicken." Consternation among waitstaff, a little scurrying, several conferences. George shrugs his shoulders quietly. "I can't make ribs in two minutes . . ."

"Wait, wait"—the waitperson in her tuxedo comes in—"they were changing their minds to ribs and arguing, when we said they couldn't do it. But it's O.K.—they changed them back when they saw the broiled bluefish."

"I do make very good fish," says George.

The second problem is that Harry sees a passing tray with very little chicken on it. Which is not in itself a problem, because there is plenty more chicken. Only somehow, the dish with not enough chicken gets lost, and Harry wanders among the tables with a plate of chicken, looking for someone who is hungry enough to want more.

"It's details, details like this, that matter," he says, as I follow him. "You don't want people thinking they've been cheated."

"Where'd you get the system of color coding the place cards?" I ask.

"You know, I don't even know?" he stops suddenly. "Maybe the Art League? I'll find out for you. I should find out for myself. It's such a great system. Now, who wants more chicken?"

Harry walks off, greeting and talking as he goes, and it is not till the end of the night, when the Batter has finally finished with the Art League and with its normal Saturday night rush out on the porch, that he gets back to me.

"That system was invented by Vickie," he says. "I should have known. Everything I don't think of, she thinks of and takes care of. You know, we couldn't have done that dinner without that system. And the extra dishes she was smart enough to know we needed. We couldn't do anything. *I* couldn't do anything. There wouldn't"—Harry stops, looking for some adequate words to say what he means—"Without Vickie, we wouldn't even be a restaurant."

MY FATHER—AND TOAST AND BUTTER

"My father—who I revere—was a tailor all his life. But all his life he was interested in life, he was interested in people," says Harry Kulkowitz. "When I went off the first summer to work as a waiter in the Catskills—did I tell you I was a waiter in the Catskills? Well, in high school that's what I did summer. He said to me and I never forgot it, remember these are working people—they work hard all year long, so they can have these two weeks in the sun. Don't take it away from them. For this once, let them be kings. That's what I tell the waitstaff. Let these people be kings. You know, we don't have a dress code —we don't run a formal restaurant. First, I don't believe in them. The restaurant is supposed to accommodate itself to you, not you to the restaurant. Second, those formal restaurants— the fancy places—are really not concentrating on being restaurants. It's theater. Like everybody growing handlebar moustaches for Victorian Sunday in Cape May. But we have people who come in here dressed up, dressed formally. We love it. We have a waiter come up with a napkin over his arm, we try to flame something and light their cigarettes every time they pick one up—the whole thing. But it's theater—we're kidding it. They know we're kidding, and they love it, too. That's just another way of making them kings.

"And that's why I'm so worried about toast and butter. Come in the kitchen and I'll show you. First, the toast is coming out on a separate plate—but there's only one separate plate for the whole table. This is a compromise, but at least you don't *have* to put the jellied toast on your omelet plate. You share a plate with everybody else at the table. Now the butter . . .

"Wait—one more important thing. You need something in

every restaurant to survive—something to fall back on when business is slow. This is a labor intensive business, and my labor costs are thirty-eight to forty percent of my gross, even in the busy season. When I open early, I expect to lose money the first month or two. So we need a cushion—for rain, for a gas shortage, for inflation. Most restaurants have a bar. We don't. We have the Carroll Villa, where we rent rooms. We thought of having a bar—but we looked and looked at restaurants with bars. First, you get a different customer. I don't mean they drink more—people bring wine here, and they drink a lot of it. But you get people who care about drinks first. And you have to have a bartender, and there's a tendency for a lot of profits to disappear in free drinks. The Villa essentially pays for the rent of the restaurant, and we don't need anything more than that. But if anybody is going into the restaurant business—I don't think you can survive without a liquor license. And without keeping an eye on your bartender. Now here"—we walk into the kitchen—"is the breakfast butter."

A large metal tray filled with ice, with a smaller tray inside filled with neatly line-up butter pats—all standing on their sides.

"The ice should keep it from melting. It's right at the pickup station—not in the refrigerator. This should solve the problem."

"Don't you think it takes up an awful lot of room on the waitstation, Harry?" says Robin Fedderman. "We move an awful lot of plates in and out of here, and it gets awful crowded when we do."

Harry considers.

"It might take up too much room," he says. "If it does, we'll change it."

So I can't tell you for sure that the butter problem has been solved permanently; if you ever go into the Mad Batter for breakfast and get your butter wrapped in golden foil, you'll know that the ice-tray solution failed—and the waitstaff is letting Harry know, once again, that they just don't like the new system.

"Well, nothing is permanent—except the problems," says

Harry. "The problems is—we are all perfectionists. And perfection is impossible in this business. *And* unless we tried to be perfect, we could never stand all the work."

We start walking out of the kitchen, and Harry turns and stops, as if he doesn't want to leave—perhaps because he likes the heat. "You know," he says, "I just realized. In all the time I talked to you, in all the stories about my life, I never told you one thing. I always wanted to own a restaurant. Just like everybody else. How could I forget it? It's so true." He waves his hand, taking in all of the busy people, all the hot and steamy air. "This is it. My fantasy. What I always wanted to do."

FIVE

BEHIND THE CHOW MEIN CURTAIN

HOW TO TELL NEW CHINESE RESTAURANTS

Somewhere in Manhattan, north of Tenth Street and south of Harlem, Liu Shao Chi (not his real name) owns and operates the kind of Chinese restaurant that could not have existed twenty years ago. The lights are low, the prices high. The walls are a dark and handsome color, the tablecloths white linen, topped with candles in brass candlesticks, an elegant vase filled with fresh flowers, glasses suitable for red or white wine—and chopsticks. There is no sugar bowl. If you drink tea with your Chinese meal (a Western practice that Liu frowns on but tolerates), you will have to take it without sugar. Sugar is not Chinese. There is no soy sauce on the table. The way Liu feels about customers who squirt soy sauce over their plate before digging in is roughly the way that a French chef feels about customers who indiscriminately layer everything, from omelet to steak Diane, with A-1 and ketchup. Only Liu seems to feel a little more intensely about it: "Americans," he says in despair, "Americans even put soy sauce on rice! This is like I come to your house and put salt on plain bread. Too weird to look at."

Liu's restaurant is open for lunch: "Very good, very adventurous customers for lunch. At dinner, some customers a little shy of some Chinese food. Maybe they like to experiment more on expense account more. We close at eleven. No four- or five-A.M. closing with drunken men from the bars. We are open eight hours a day, we work ten or twelve hours, because we must cut and prepare the food. Chinese food takes much slicing and preparation. We do it after lunch. We don't serve food while we are slicing—'doing side work' we call it. That way we concentrate, we do it right.

"I have very good customers. I like them. We speak the same language. I spend time talking to my old customers. I am the chef here. I have an assistant chef who is very good, very talented. And I trained. So he can take over. Part of my job is to walk out in the dining room and say hello. Two or three times a night. More. How is the store coming or how is the painting going I ask. How is the neighborhood doing. I wanted this level customer. Very sophisticated, very gentle, very mild temper. In a suburban restaurant, you get people who don't know what they're eating. And they give you a lot of trouble."

Liu takes me back to the kitchen to show me how it is organized. It is completely different than a kitchen in a French or American restaurant. First of all, the stove is different. Chinese stoves are lower, and without burners or the flat top of the classic French restaurant stove. Instead there are two holes in the metal top for woks to sit on, one wok slightly larger than the other but both smaller than most of the woks sold in American department stores. Both the woks have fat handles on them, hollow-core steel wrapped in a tight fabric coil so they can be lifted easily no matter how hot they get. Water runs over the metal top constantly, from a hidden pipe in the front of the stove to a trough at the back and then down the kitchen drain.

"It cools the stove," says Liu. "You must be able to turn the gas up very high. Flames shoot out from under the bottom of the wok, cook everything in a minute or so. If we did not have water in the summer, it would be two hundred degrees in here. American restaurants don't have water on the stove?"

No, I say, they just heat the whole top.

"They must have air conditioning?"

No, they can't, because that would cool the food on the plate too fast.

Liu looks at me in disbelief.

"They suffer? For what? Tell them get a Chinese stove. Work is hard enough without suffering too."

That might be a good idea—I hung around through several nights in Liu's kitchen and it is much much cooler than a normal restaurant kitchen. And the chef doesn't get that heat-glazed look around the eyes or the kitchen flush about the face. In fact, as quickly as the Chinese chef works—and he turns out food at least as fast as any Western cook—he never even seems to come close to working up a sweat.

All around us preparation is going on. An assistant chef, who is wearing a T-shirt that says UCLA because that is the school he graduated from, is simultaneously removing the wings and the skin from chickens. He takes one of those razor-sharp Chinese cleaver-shaped knives, turns the chicken on its side and grasps the chicken wing firmly in his left hand. In one quick movement he draws a line with the blade along the ridge of the breastbone, cuts in a little deeper to sever the wing from the body and moves the blade around down the back of the chicken, pulling at the bone with his other hand. The wing and half the skin comes off, all in one piece. He turns the chicken over, takes off the other wing and the rest of the skin just as quickly. Then he removes the legs, straightens them out flat and, with what seem like two slight shifts of the blade, simply removes drumstick and thigh bone in one piece. The breast comes off in two pieces, in two quick movements, and what was a chicken is now white meat, dark meat, wings and a carcass.

"Takes about one minute for a chicken," says Liu. "My assistant chef is very fast. Trained by me, in America. This is the new kitchen worker in Chinese restaurants. The new immigrants are from the city—they know more food, they learn here very quick. Takes one year to learn. We use dark meat in Szechuan chicken, the breast in sesame chicken because it is the most tender. Everything else goes in the stock. The little part of the breast next to the bone is the tenderest part and we leave it on because it goes in the stock to cook. Then is removed to become an appetizer you see in many Szechuan restaurants—pon pon chicken—slices of breast meat with a sesame paste and hot pepper sauce. Very good and now very popular with my customers. We will marinate our chicken in flavor depending on the dish, and very often we marinate meat in egg white. I think you do not do this in American kitchens? But it makes things very tender. You can tenderize any meat this way. Egg white and a little water and cornstarch and sherry. Beat them up and marinate overnight. This is the only way to get the texture of Chinese food in your home cooking. We bone fresh ham too—the whole leg of pork. I will show you."

The assistant chef laughs aloud as Liu takes off his neat brown suit jacket and hangs it over the kitchen door. The assistant chef brings a big pork leg from the walk-in refrigerator, and Liu takes up the cleaver, talking as he works.

"Maybe I slow down," Liu says. "But I am very fast." He peels off an outside layer of fat, inserts the blade of the cleaver at a joint, moves his hand and takes out the entire shoulder bone, a big oddly curved socket.

"You have to know where the bone goes," Liu says, "and where the knife goes."

A line drawn down the center of the leg exposes the whole bone, which is then removed in one more swift and sure movement. Then the hock is taken off, the meat sliced deftly here and there so it will lie flat, fat is trimmed off and three quick piles are made.

Liu points to each of the piles. "Most tender, tender, and only for grinding and putting in steam dumpling . . . Finish boning." He looks at his watch. "Little over two minutes. I am still fast. I learn this in restaurants where we bone and cook lunch at once, so you have to be fast."

The delighted assistant chef laughingly says something in Chinese, and Liu laughs too.

"Yes," he says. "You have to know where the fingers go.

Otherwise . . ." He shows me the index finger on his left hand —which has a scar running all around it from one side of the fingernail to the other. "Otherwise you cut off top of your finger instead of top of the leg. One more reason I like to do side work after lunch in my restaurant. We work fast. But we don't have to try to work too fast."

EVERYTHING IS DIFFERENT. MANY THINGS ARE THE SAME

Though everything about a Chinese restaurant kitchen is different, many things are essentially the same as in a Western kitchen.

The stove is different. Not only does water flow across the top, there are also two long water spigots, which look like half-inch stainless-steel pipes, on the back of the stove. They are arranged on a swivel, and when the chef swivels them out straight, they turn on automatically, dropping water exactly where the wok is.

"I don't see why everyone does not have these kind of spigots," says Liu. "You turn them on even with a ladle, you turn them off even with your hands full by just pushing them, they can't drip or run when they are not supposed to. Why would anybody want those funny little handles on spigots?"

Though the spigots are different, Chinese chefs clean out their woks almost exactly the way Western chefs clean out their sauté pans. Westerners, when they switch from one meat to another or have cooked a sauce in a pan beforehand, simply give the pan a quick scrub with a kitchen steel—the curly stainless-steel ball that looks like a chromed version of Orphan Annie curls. Since everything is cooked in clarified butter that is enough to get any leftover taste out of the pan. Chinese chefs use water and either the same curly steel or a stiff wire-bristle brush—they fill the wok with hot water, scrub and then simply dump the water over the side where it is flushed away with the rest of the stove water. The whole operation is done in a second, and every trace of sauce is gone.

As in Western kitchens, there is a cold side. But the Chinese cold side is a stand which holds a series of sunken little metal pots—like a steam table, except that it is refrigerated. In the pots are the vegetables of the evening, bean sprouts, snow peas, and different small portions of marinated meat and shrimp. When the waiter hands in the order, the assistant chef takes out the vegetables and puts them on the plate they will be served on, arranging four or five plates on a shelf in front of the cold trays.

The chef stands at the stove with the woks in front of him. Beside him is the Chinese version of the French *mise en place*—a series of small bowls with a succession of sauces and spices. The number of bowls varies with the restaurant. At Tang's, where much of the cooking is Szechuan, it includes: sugar; salt; vinegar; a cornstarch and water mix; hot pepper sauce; ginger shaved into shreds; sherry; soy sauce; garlic; a thick, dark, Chinese hoisin sauce; a thinner sauce, just as dark and slightly hot, called "Peking sauce"; tomato puree; oriental sesame oil. The chef uses his long-handled utensil—something that looks like a cross between a scoop, a deep spoon and a ladle—to dip from these bowls according to the recipe. It is done as quickly as the water cleaning, and with as little hesitation—but it means that unlike most Western restaurants, where sauces are kept in steam tables, all Chinese sauces are assembled instantaneously and to order.

On either side of the stove are the two other indispensable pieces of kitchen equipment: a deep-fat fryer on the right, a big twenty-gallon pot of chicken soup simmering away on the left.

"We have two fryers," says Liu. "One is for ordinary deep fry. Egg roll, crispy duck. The other is for Chinese cooking we call 'raw in oil.' Only in old-fashioned Cantonese restaurants you get simple stir-fry food. We do almost everything raw in oil. Watch. We do . . . Szechuan shrimp!"

The assistant chef quickly pulls vegetables from their refrigerated bins and hands them to the chef on the serving plate.

The chef scoops a bit of oil in his wok, drops in the vegetables, a bit of sugar, salt, sherry, tomato, garlic, hot pepper sauce and soy sauce. He turns the handle and the stove throws flames an inch or two high around the bottom of the wok. No change in kitchen temperature is noticeable though we are standing at his shoulder, but the water running across the top of the stove begins to steam, and the vegetables and liquid in the wok flash suddenly to the boil. The assistant chef dumps eight shrimp into a deep-fry basket and then into a deep fryer for no longer than thirty seconds. The shrimp have not even changed color when they come out of the fryer, are given a shake to drain them and dumped onto the wok. Another stir or two with the ladle, a bit of sesame oil "for flavor," a half scoop of chicken stock to bind the sauce together—and the entree goes back onto the serving platter and the waiter pickup counter in one easy motion. With another, the chef turns the spigot to the "on" position, the water boils and steams as it hits the wok. He scrubs quickly with the big brush, tilts the pan to empty the water, turns off the gas. It takes longer to read this than it takes to do it. The effect is of one furious burst of cooking, and the kitchen returning, like the water and the gas jet, to a quiet "off" position.

"This is very fast cooking," says Liu. "You never get the texture of this shrimp at home without raw in oil. And without egg-white marinade. It tastes . . . tender. Not this tough shrimp like potatoes in Western cooking. American cooking is sometimes odd"—Liu shakes his head—"I like Western restaurants and much Western food. But I came to this country first to go to college and I have an apartment with an American and he cooks in the kitchen. He cooks vegetables"—Liu shakes his head—"he cooks them in so much water . . . so long . . . so long *they change color!* I cannot believe it. They change color! Then—he throws the water away! I tell him when you cook you eat the vegetables, if you want, but I throw them away. I drink the water instead. There is all the taste, all the vitamins—all the food. 'You don't even eat vegetables,' I told him, 'you eat the bones of vegetables.'"

WHAT'S WRONG WITH MSG?

Many Americans get a bad reaction from MSG, I say to Liu.

"Many Americans?" says Liu. "Many Chinese, too. Me. I hate that stuff. We don't have it in my restaurant. Many Chinese chefs say that and still use a little. But I get sick from it and we do not have any. Any. I get sweats, red face, dizzy, a hung-over feeling—the worst time, I was driving from San Francisco to L.A. and in San Francisco I had a meal in a famous Chinese restaurant. Then I start to drive and in half an hour I am so sick I have to stop, stay in a motel. I told my wife then—I will never have this MSG in my restaurant. I have to be careful in Chinese restaurants and say I am allergic, and even then sometimes you can't trust some places. They lie and stick in MSG anyhow.

"We don't need that stuff here. The chicken stock is our MSG. Some of it goes in every sauce. It is the base of all our soups. We make it with the bones, starting the first of the week. It cooks and chef skims it for four hours before we open. It is used all night long. At the end of the night, you must bring it to a hard boil. Then not touch it. Next morning, already it is solid, concentrated, like a jelly. We start it again, add more bones. Use it again. Boil again. The third day we cook with it but it does not come to a boil at the end of the night. We throw it all away and start a new soup the next day. You must change the soup or it spoils, but you must keep the soup long enough for the taste. Western cooking is bone cooking. You cook the meat on the bone. We take out the bone, cook the flavor out of it. Then we make the meat as tender as possible and add flavor with the stock.

"This is the way I run my kitchen, the way most new restaurants outside Chinatown run their kitchen. I buy small, three-pound chickens, the tenderest. You can taste the difference. A Chinatown restaurant might buy capon—lots more meat on the bone but this is tougher meat and too juicy for me. It does not cook as well, Chinese style."

CHINESE WAITERS

"Two things about Chinese waiters. Lots of customers give them trouble. Especially in the suburban restaurants. And lots of Chinese waiters are very educated—men and women with masters and doctorate, sometimes they are just working to get enough money for English lessons and they are too proud to serve you. Lots of Chinatown waiters I have trouble with myself. They don't talk nice! I don't want to hear this when I am spending my money. But these are the old waiters, like old diner waiters—very gruff, very fast, 'no substitutes.' They worked for twenty years and nobody is going to change them.

"You know, in Chinatown they don't even figure tips on the bill by percent—you know waiters are always estimating their tips before they get them. But in Chinatown they never think about the size of the bill, just the size of the table—they figure fifty cents a head. And usually that is all they get. Here, my waiters average seventeen percent of the bill—I have good customers. And I have good waiters. I tell them, the tips are there, you have to work for it. In Chinatown you run for it—if the place is big, a waiter has thirty tables. You try to hire more waiters so he has less tables, he will quit. He needs thirty tables to make a living. He runs. He comes in the back with the dishes, he pours them in . . . like trash into a dumpster. That's why you see such thick dishes in old-style restaurants. They have to be able to take all that crashing around. Here we have thin china, all matching, very nice, with little figures holding good luck ideograms. And my waiters do not have to move as fast. Still I have breakage. Chips and cracks. I have five cases of little chips and cracks in my basement. I can't serve it. It looks too good to throw away. I should throw it away. I keep it. Stubbornly.

"Sometimes the restaurant is small. And then the waiters have to move you fast so they can keep the food cheap and the tips small and have so much turnover they still make some money. I had a waiter start here who worked in a small Chinatown restaurant. People stand in line outside. They get a menu when they come in the door. They have to order before they even get to the table. And when they sit down, the food sits down with them. And no conversation at these tables. He tells me the waiters have to come around to make sure you are eating. He goes up to table and says, 'You finish, leave. You not finish, eat. No talk.' I told him he better never do this to my customers. Besides, lots of time the person talking at the tables is me.

"Chopsticks. We set up chopsticks, but all Chinese restaurants have them and you can tell a lot about the place from the chopsticks. Expensive restaurants use ivory chopsticks—imitation ivory, made of plastic. I tried that here. But too many people took them home, and they are too expensive. Now I use wood chopsticks. I lose them too. You have to lose chopsticks. But instead of a dollar a pair they are ten cents a pair. Some restaurants use bamboo chopsticks. Only one cent a pair. But they curl in the dishwasher. You know them if you use chopsticks. They look like bowlegs. Like trying to eat with a hoop. And they stain from the food. You can see that too. The tips darken. Most unappetizing. And besides that, they pick up taste from the detergent in the wash machine. If I had some, I would show you. But try it yourself when you see bowleg chopsticks. Just put the tip to your nose and smell. Just like Lo-Bax detergent. Sometimes like bleach, if they try to get them white again."

THE REAL CHINESE FOOD

I ask Liu about the difficulties many Americans have getting authentic Chinese food. There is even a famous linguist who has a tiny piece of paper he carries with him to Chinese restaurants. It says "Bring me what is on that table over there" in ideograms. Whenever he sees a party of Chinese eating something that looks delicious and exotic, he shows his paper to the waiter and points. That way he gets real Chinese food.

"Maybe he doesn't like the real Chinese food," laughs Liu.

"I will tell you about that. I said that the best Chinese restaurants are outside Chinatown. Better waiters, trained to be nicer. Better ingredients. Better chefs. But only in Chinatown, only in New York and San Francisco Chinatown you can depend on Chinese customers. Everywhere else, even midtown Manhattan, you depend on Americans. Some Americans are very sophisticated about Chinese food. They use chopsticks correctly. They like dim sum. They are expert at chewing the meat off roast chicken feet . . . You like it too? My four-year-old daughter too. It is delicious, and good children food. But only in New York can you serve dim sum. Dim sum is Chinese tea food, for the morning or afternoon. In China there are always people around to eat dim sum. In America, everybody has to work. They get an hour for lunch, they can't spend the two hours it takes to sit through a dim sum serving. Except in New York. Chinatown is near SoHo, where they have many artists, painters who can sit around all day if they want and maybe they work nights.

"We used to have Chinese dessert. Bride cake, winter melon cake, noodle cake. We sell a few portions but Americans just don't like Chinese dessert. Not even these, all made by my wife. We took them off the menu. And now instead of dessert I give you orange quartered up. No fortune cookie. I have never seen them till I come to the United States. There are no fortune cookies in China! None. No such thing. Where did they find this food for Americans here?

"Sometimes Chinese come in here and ask for the Chinese menu. We say, no, we have only one menu—we serve the same food to everybody. They open their eyes and stare sometimes —but they come back. Our food is Chinese.

"But we cannot have some food. In my father's restaurant, I give you an example. We had beef with shrimp sauce. This is a taste delicious to Chinese. The shrimp are dried in the sun. Until they smell. The smell is strong and the taste is strong. Many cuisines have this smell and this taste and it is always hard to get used to. Remember the first time you ever taste ripe cheese? Roquefort? Many people never get used to that taste. There are Americans who can't stand Roquefort.

"Americans are not used to this taste on beef and shrimp and we tell them it is a very strong taste. We warn them they will not like it. Some people change their order, but other people, if you warn them, this is what they must order. We bring it. Nine out of ten do not finish it, and one of them, even after we warn them, insists the meat is spoiled and sends it back to the kitchen. One out of ten finishes. We cannot eat all this beef and shrimp. We cannot afford to make it for the one in ten Americans who likes it. It must come off the menu.

"You have to think about your customers when you think about food," Liu continues. "I have an idea that most other restaurants do not. I use fresh American vegetables. Traditional recipes, but I change the ingredients. This is only sensible. In China, you use the best, in America you should use the best too. So in my restaurant you find asparagus in season. This is wonderful with spicy beef. You do not find bok choy all the time. June and July bok choy is excellent. Otherwise, in America, it tastes bitter. So I use it in season. Broccoli flowers are a very good vegetable with Chinese food, and we get very good broccoli in winter.

"Fish is more difficult. Some fish is wonderful for Chinese cooking. Black bass, sea trout, carp. But I must call the fish markets before I go and ask what kind of fish they have. My fish must be fresh. And sometimes I get up in the morning five A.M., go all the way down to the market after I call and they say they have lots of fresh fish. And they have lots of fresh butterfish. I cannot cook this in a Chinese kitchen. Bluefish I had on the menu. But I was not satisfied. I did not find the virtue of the fish for cooking. And I did not want to do one of those steam fish with soy sauce and vegetables you find on American menus. Called Orientale, with an extra *e*. So I took bluefish off until I conduct further experiments. There is a wide range of much food in America and Chinese cooking has many techniques, so this is a challenge for a Chinese chef to combine them. Very exciting food results. Sometimes.

"One problem in my restaurant is . . . stealing. All restaurants have this, and I think it is not my regular customers. But many people must have a souvenir of a Chinese restaurant.

Chopsticks I do not mind, though it means I cannot use the best chopsticks. Flowers I do not mind. A couple dollars' worth a night. Vases I mind. I bought these vases when I started and they do not make them any more. I bought plenty, I thought. But I have no more. And if you look carefully at the first four tables of my restaurant, you see that the vases are different. How do they steal a vase full of flowers? It goes in the pocketbooks. I worked in a restaurant one time where a woman took a soy sauce dispenser, full of soy sauce, and just put it in her pocketbook. What can you do? But we had this one waiter who was very funny. Always making us laugh. He goes up to the woman when she is at the cashier and says, 'Oh, madam, excuse me, you have something spilled on your pocketbook.' It hangs from her shoulder, so he just takes it, turns it upside down, and wipes the bottom. All the waiters, the cashier, everybody is trying not to laugh. The woman looks at him horrified but can say nothing. I think she did not steal again from the next Chinese restaurant."

SIX

WHY MCDONALD'S SUCCEEDED SO WELL

AND WHY ALL FAST FOOD IS IN TROUBLE

McDonald's is the great American food chain, still leading after all these years. But it isn't just a food chain. McDonald's is the largest child-oriented advertiser on television. Each and every dollar of its TV budget seems to be spent trying to convince the kids to take Mom and Dad out to eat. Food is fun at McDonald's, and it even has funny faces—from Big Mac to Egg McMuffin to the clown with the permanent painted smile, Ronald McDonald, who personifies the commercial friendliness of the whole chain.

Ronald loves kids—and kids love Ronald back. A recent survey of American children showed that 96 percent of them recognized Ronald McDonald on sight. That's more than recognized any American President, from George Washington to Ronald Reagan; more than recognized Uncle Sam or the Easter Bunny or Sesame Street's Big Bird; more than recognized any other real or fictional character, living or dead—except Santa Claus.

Would lovable Ronald steer kids wrong about food? Why, he cares about kids so much he doesn't even serve vegetables. And everything he does serve seems especially designed to please palates that are only a step away from Pablum. It is all bland, and soft, and vaguely sweet. The basic McDonald's product—1.6 ounces of ground beef on a specially sugary bun —tastes like a full-color computer printout of a hamburger printed on wadded rice paper. And it has all the texture of a peanut butter and jelly sandwich.

Many nutritionists believe that friends like Ronald are worse than enemies. A meal at McDonald's is, essentially, a super-polysaturated cholesterol bomb. The combination of Big Mac, chocolate shake, and french fries is high in carbohydrates, close to zero in Vitamin A and C and contains 1,089 calories, about half the limit for children under 10 recommended by the Federal Food and Nutrition Council.

Feed your child three times a day at McDonald's, and in no time he'll be overweight, toothless and a victim of beriberi and/or scurvy. To say nothing of being scarred emotionally when he discovers that Ronald loves him—but only until he reaches puberty. McDonald's hates teenagers.

So there are special McDonald's out in richest suburbia where you can use a toy telephone to talk to the recorded voice of Ronald McDonald—and watch yourself on closed-circuit TV at the same time. But there is not a single McDonald's where you can make a telephone call to the outside world. Or buy a pack of cigarettes, a candy bar, a newspaper, or a stick of gum. There is not a single McDonald's where you can play a jukebox, a pinball or a video game machine. Because all McDonald's owners are forbidden by the terms of their contract from providing those usual restaurant amenities. Amenities only encourage teenagers, says the central office sternly. Teenagers hang out together. They don't spend money. They don't bring Mom and Dad. So Ronald makes sure that there's no inducement for them to do anything but eat up and go out-

WHY MCDONALD'S SUCCEEDED SO WELL

side somewhere, hopefully to reproduce and come back soon as parents.

But McDonald's is the biggest food chain in America, because it is better than lots of American restaurant food. Better than most in its price class. And it is not necessarily the enemy of childhood health.

No one—least of all Ronald—says you should eat all your meals at McDonald's. McDonald's sells itself as fun food—a new American tradition which has no more to do with balanced nutrition than pizza pie or ball-park hot dogs. Restaurants have never been places to go if you're looking for vitamins. In fact, if you fed your child three meals a day in the most expensive and elegant French or Continental restaurants you could find, he'd probably wind up with every disease he'd get at McDonald's—plus gout from all the wine sauces.

The chief difference between McDonald's and other restaurants is not that McDonald's delivers poor nutrition, but that it delivers what it advertises and does it consistently.

How many times have you taken some friends to a restaurant you've spent weeks praising—only to find that the spectacular meal you promised has magically turned into a parade of what looks like warmed up leftovers? Either the chef left, or the owner took a vacation, or you have simply stumbled on one of those numerous and unlovable restaurants that are good one day and execrable the next.

McDonald's is dependent on a system which allows no room for human error. There is a timer that tells the (usually teenage) cook when to flip the hamburger patties, and a company rule that prevents food from standing around unsold. (An unordered hamburger must be thrown out after ten minutes; a pot of coffee after thirty minutes.) Whatever they may say about the overall food value of a McDonald's meal, nutritionists give McDonald's *meat* very good marks. All McDonald's hamburgers must be all beef and contain no more than 18.9 percent fat—a ratio that is much better than the 20 percent fat found in many expensive restaurant hamburgers. Only steer short-plate beef or chuck steak can be used in McDonald's hamburgers—no heart, lungs, tripe, cheek, head, flavor boosters, preservatives, protein additives, soy extenders, fillers or cereals. Look at a McDonald's burger and look at a typical diner burger and you can see the difference, even without tasting it: McDonald's has none of those squiggly little white bits of aorta or esophagus in it, no bits of ground up gristle, no breadcrumb-and-egg mix.

It's easy to attack McDonald's—but remember, what you're really attacking is American restaurants and American eating habits in general. And it's easy to defend McDonald's—as among the best of a pretty bad lot.

I review restaurants for a living, and whenever I describe one that is particularly bad, I get a letter from the owner telling me how long he has been in business (never less than thirty-five years), how early he gets up (never later than 4 A.M.), how he delivers the kind of food he knows from long experience that his customers want (ancient seafood, overcooked meat, string beans steam-tabled so long they look like olive drab spaghetti). And winding up with the all-purpose excuse— "You can always have a bad experience in a restaurant . . . We have a new chef . . . My most experienced help is on vacation . . ."

I know you can have a bad experience in most restaurants, but I don't see why you should pay to take that chance. And if the owner knows that his chef is sick or his most important people are on vacation, so the food is going to be worse— shouldn't he at least give us a discount? If he doesn't and since he charges by the meal, shouldn't he expect to be judged by the meal? If experience guaranteed good performance, Joe DiMaggio would still be playing center field—instead of selling Mr. Coffee.

In no other business that I know of is there so much suffering as allegedly goes into the preparation of two hundred or so meals in an old-fashion French bas cuisine restaurant. In no other occupation is the physical condition or mental outlook of the worker supposed to determine and excuse bad performance. Actors play comedy minutes after they are informed that their nearest and dearest have died. Chefs, however, are temperamental.

I know chefs are temperamental. I've worked with chefs. Short-order cooks are temperamental. I've worked with several who could give an ordinary workaday chef lessons in all-round unreasonability. I've worked with truck drivers. Truck drivers are unreasonable; truck drivers are temperamental. But they drive the trucks.

At McDonald's, they make the hamburgers.

This is partly because the McDonald's franchise owners are almost exactly the opposite of the typical bas cuisine owners. They are new to the business—have worked their way up to where they have the price of a franchise and are doing something that has nothing to do with food or food service. No thirty-five years' experience. Instead, new owners take a two-week course at McDonald's Hamburger University—that is actually what it's called.

McDonald's workers are high school students, college kids, mothers with a few hours free, anyone so unskilled or inexperienced or oppressed that they are willing to work for the minimum wage. McDonald's does not hire experienced workers. And because of its salary scale, it does not keep workers long enough for them to be experienced—the typical McDonald's owner can expect a 100 percent turnover in staff every six months. So they are always breaking in a new chef—who never gets enough experience to become temperamental. They are required to meet McDonald's standards—so they are not free to decide that their particular customers actually like hamburgers a day old or their coffee reboiled. And as a result, it is almost impossible to have a really bad experience at McDonald's. The food may be bland, but it never gives you the horrors.

If all this sounds like I'm in favor of mass-produced food and against old world attitudes of individual loving care—well, all I can say is that at McDonald's prices, in America, we don't have that choice. Most restaurants produce mass food under any number of disguises. At least McDonald's is honest about it. And honesty does pay.

There are new problems with McDonald's, and with all the other chains, however. Some of the problems are tied up with gasoline prices. One suburban housewife, interviewed in the New York *Times* about how one or another of the many gasoline shortages had changed her life, said, "Well, for one thing we send out for pizza now a lot more. The Pizza Hut delivers. We have to drive to McDonald's." A remark that must have struck terror in the hearts of all fast-food franchise owners.

For another thing, McDonald's, like all chains, is bothered more and more by owners who do not live up to their contracts. It is very easy to find a McDonald's outside of the lunch and dinner rushes, where hamburgers are left much more than ten minutes in those little holding trays. Worse yet, some chains have decided that the bother of training people to turn hamburgers over at the sound of a bell is not worth it. Some chains now have hamburgers in cold storage already cooked, and they are merely microwaved to order. This is not fast food and not fun food—it is simply vending machine food, with high school students instead of machines. All this is catching up with our fast-food franchises, and they are starting to grow a little tired. Profits sag, growth slows, and the food gets worse.

Even more frightening—the baby-boom generation is grown up. What will happen to Ronald in a society where there are less and less children? Will he have to take off the clown mask and start treating his customers like grownups?

I doubt it. But the White Tower restaurants were a chain that started with a simple idea—put your fast-food restaurant right near a public transportation stop. And the explosion of car ownership after World War II killed them off. Maybe our new franchise food will turn out to be a temporary by-product of the baby boom and cheap gas.

But two bits of information will help you eat better while you wait to see what will happen to all those convenience restaurants.

The first is simple. To call your product a hamburger, you must by law, everywhere in America, make it of nothing but beef—no extenders. If you use any extender at all, the hamburger can only be called a "beef patty." Keeping this in mind when you're reading signs and menus will at least keep you from paying meat prices for soyburgers.

And if you go into a McDonald's in off hours and find lots of little boxes already filled, waiting under the warming lamps, ask for a hamburger without ketchup. That way the counterperson has to call it in special, and you get a hamburger cooked to your very own order. Almost no other restaurant chain will take that trouble. If you like ketchup on your hamburger, just ask for an order of fries and you'll get a little plastic pack of ketchup on the side for the asking. And a lot of hot freshly made and sweetened food that is mediocre at best—and the best food, in most places, for miles around.

SEVEN

AN ALTERNATIVE EDEN

"The major influences on my restaurants and my life were Jane Jacobs and Phil Pochoda. Jane Jacobs wrote a book called *The Death and Life of Great American Cities,* and in there she talked about the neighborhood candy store and its role in defining the lives of the people in the neighborhood—making a neighborhood. Phil Pochoda was a teacher of mine at the University of Pennsylvania, who taught political sociology, which I took because I was a naive do-gooder. And it was my first introduction to political philosophy. Phil gave me the first idea that it was possible to have a framework through which to look at society—and criticize society. Jane Jacobs is the no-nonsense city planner. Radical theory in the sixties, that helped me realize who the restaurants were going to be designed for . . . And . . . And I always liked to cook."

Meet Steve Poses, laughing lightly as he talks about the theory and history of his Philadelphia restaurants. He is owner and entrepreneur of Frög, the 16th Street Bar and Grill, the Commissary, a takeout convenience food store called the Market and two branches of a restaurant called Eden—which may become the country's first alternative fast-food chain. Steve is large, bearded, casually dressed, and sitting at his desk in a third-story office over the building that houses the Commissary, the bakery for all his restaurants, a thriving catering business and dozens of management workers, in cooking whites or street clothes, who move busily from office to office.

A little history of Steve to begin with—personal, political and business history:

"I grew up in Yonkers, New York, in a typical upper middle class Jewish family. I came to Philadelphia to study architecture at the University of Pennsylvania and discovered that I couldn't draw very well . . . I thought I couldn't be an architect unless I could draw. I later found out that the one thing didn't have anything to do with the other—but everybody at Penn thought it did. Luckily. So I decided to go into urban planning, and there was no urban planning major for undergraduates so I took sociology. And got caught up in the whole ferment of the sixties, the antiwar movement.

"When I graduated I was program director of the Committee for a Sane Nuclear Policy, and I started looking around for a job. I taught for a while in a school for troubled children, and then got a physical deferment from the Army for hemorrhoids. So to make a living, I got a job as busboy and glass polisher at what was at the time the only *haute cuisine* restaurant in the city of Philadelphia. And I saw royalty at work. And I didn't like it.

"My own restaurants are a reaction against that kind of class and caste distinction in restaurants. When I opened Frög, I didn't do it to become a great restaurant. I thought it would be a kind of extension of the coffeehouses of the fifties. A place where people could discuss the issues of the day. Hopefully, come up with solutions to the issues of the day. And a place where the guy who owned it happened to like to cook. I picked a neighborhood of young professionals in center-city Philadelphia—one that no one had defined as a neighborhood. And I decided that my restaurant would function like the corner candy store. That's Jane Jacobs. And I also decided that it would be a corner candy store not only for that neighborhood, but for all the people who were part of the baby boom and moving into the professions after school—a corner candy store for our generation. That's Phil Pochoda. A friend of mine and I—he'd just got out of architecture school—literally hammered together Frög in about a month. It was a storefront restaurant, and we filled the window with plants—everybody was getting plants then and that was part of the sign of our generation.

"And there was nobody to tell us how to run a restaurant. You know, all of us who started working in Frög were like our customers, from the American upper middle class. We didn't have any cooking traditions. I learned to respect food from my mother, but I certainly didn't learn to cook from her. We didn't know that certain tastes don't usually go together and we experimented. We didn't have an ethnic tradition. We had . . . Time-Life cookbooks—that's my food tradition, food from all around the world. And at the expensive restaurant where I'd worked, a lot of the kitchen staff was from Thailand—don't ask me why. Probably some Thai student got a job and told his friends, and they got jobs and stayed on. Those staff dinners were a big influence on my own cooking—lots of Thai curries, nuts in the food, stir fries . . . We used to, in fact, have an entree on our menu called Staff Dinner, after those old Thai dinners I remember. But I forget what it was now—curried beef and stir-fried vegetables. Probably.

"I remember on Frög's first menu we had an omelet with snails and walnuts. Which was unusual. And a brochette—everybody said, 'Wow! What's a brochette?' And stir fries. And I was the chef. The cook. I don't remember much of the first couple of years, because they went by in a fog. Of steam from the steamer and smoke from the broiler.

"Well, times change. We used to say, if we could just do six thousand dollars a week, it'd be terrific. And when we did, it was terrific. But looking back I realize that I wouldn't have been satisfied in the past eight years just to be behind the stove of a six-thousand-dollar-gross restaurant. I wanted my restaurants to be more, a place where people talk. They do talk. I'm sure they talk more about . . . what do people talk about now? . . . soap operas . . . than they do about whether or not what our government is doing in El Salvador is necessarily the right thing to do. And that's fine with me. I can do something else about Reagan. I'm still politically active. The politics have changed a little, maybe—maybe I've just found new ways of doing the same thing. When you leave, I have an appointment with a guy from the Democratic National Committee who wants to arrange a local fund raiser . . . That's what I do about El Salvador, now.

"As for the restaurants, you know I was interested in city planning. I have no doubt I've had more impact on this city with my restaurants than I'd ever have had as a drawing-board planner. A restaurant *is* like a candy store—it did help define a neighborhood and a generation—and my job . . . I create, help create institutions. I'm talking about small institutions that give people I know—people in our extended family—a chance to exercise their talents and their creativity. And . . . we happen to be good at making good food and presenting it attractively.

"Old Frög opened in 1973, full of plants, full of the energy of the sixties. New Frög opened in 1980—no plants, more austere, more formal, more like the successful professionals that our market has grown into. Other things have changed, too. I tend to be more political than the new members of the staff. That would've been unheard of in 1973—for the older, more successful person to be more politically active. But it's true. I politicize my staff now.

"In between old Frög and new Frög, we opened the Commissary, which is a cafeteria, with a cafeteria line. But with things nobody ever dared to try in a cafeteria. Homemade pasta cooked in front of you. Omelets made while you watch and stuffed with your choice of ingredients—omelets made the French way, by shaking the pan in one direction and stirring in another in a French omelet pan, rolled onto the plate . . . If you can't figure out how to do it from the directions in your cookbook, come in and order an omelet at Commissary—you not only get good food, you get a demonstration.

"We had already been aggressive with wines in Frög, especially with California boutique wines. Commissary pushed a little harder. We had three or four wines-of-the-day. We marked the bottles up double—a good restaurant price—but on a sliding scale, so you paid two times retail if the wine cost me less than ten dollars, but you might only pay twenty-two dollars if the wine cost me fifteen. We sold the wines-of-the-day by the glass—a big glass. Two or three dollars. We sold a lot of wines. People would come in here to taste three or four wines, before deciding to buy any. We had very good desserts, we had big salad entrees, classic French fish soups, stir fries . . .

"You see, you have to look at the demographics. The middle and upper middle classes, who are—let's face it—our market, never really liked McDonald's. McDonald's was successful not because they liked the food, but because they liked the quickness. We were convinced that people would pay a little more if they could have really good food just as fast, and we were convinced that we could have a cafeteria line staffed with people who really cared about food. We wanted people who had respect for the customer, respect for food, respect for the preparation that went into it. We knew we had those people on our staff.

"Only"—he laughs—"that's not really how it happened. You do have to look at the demographics, and there are a lot of busy professionals who want quick food. We did have a staff of people who had the same kind of respect for good food as those professionals do. But—actually a lot of that is just hindsight, justification, rationalization . . . for something I just thought it would be fun to do. It's a challenge. A ball-buster.

"Here's how it happened.

"We were spending twenty thousand dollars a year in linen costs at Frög. And we've always had a reputation for good desserts. So I thought I'd look around for a building, or a floor, where I could have a bakery in front and a couple of washing machines in the back and save that twenty thousand. Or at least part of it. Then I thought I might as well have a retail bakery in front. Then this building came up for sale, and I took it, then I took the plans to my architect friend—actually he and his wife were camping in Tennessee, and I had to track them down, and sitting around on a picnic table in the middle of a National Forest with Sophie and Eddie, we took a pencil and figured out the Commissary. Actually, the place was too big for just a bakery and laundry, so . . . I'd always thought about cafeteria food and how it could be better. And it was really a matter of just taking space and filling it up with ideas.

"Then after Commissary was a success, we started Eden. It's really the same demographics. Eden was designed to be a lunch place and quick early dinner for the workers in the highrise office buildings. It had a cafeteria line, and it had a simplified Commissary menu. The trouble with Commissary is that it's talent-intensive. You need a lot of very well-trained people. We start all our new people in the Commissary, because in a very short period of time you learn a lot about food and about our way of cooking food. We wanted to compete with fast-food places and to do that we had to have people working in the restaurant who were entry-level people. We got lots of students, and with students we expected lots of turnover —and we couldn't teach all of them how to make an omelet.

"But think about a deep fryer. The reason a deep fryer is so essential to fast-food chains is that it's so simple. You take a young kid, show him how to put food in the fry basket and lower it in the oil: he pushes a timer at the same time and when the bell rings he takes it out. No problem about cooking. Well, deep frying is unhealthy, it's not a good way to treat food, it's high in calories, it has nothing to do with the way that the middle class and upper middle class cook at home. We have a steamer. It's a convection steamer, and it works the same way as a fryer. All day long in Eden we're steaming— chicken breasts and fish fillets. The only thing that changes from day to day is the sauce we put on them.

"We need one highly trained person for Eden—to make the sauces and the soups and to oversee the dressings for the salads. All the rest of the work is traditional kitchen work— traditional kitchen prep work. Chopping greens, slicing vegetables, with a lot of respect for greens and vegetables, of course. We don't want to have a system that makes people not care about food. We want a system that works. Students can get into food, if it's good food. They can feel good about serving an attractive plate, and they can learn how to sauce a chicken breast or a fillet of bluefish or rockfish. I could never duplicate the Commissary—the Commissary is designed to take advantage of the talents we know we have. But I can duplicate Edens—we now have a new one, even more interesting, in the big concrete superdorm for foreign students called International House at the University of Pennsylvania. You have to come and see it."

I get the feeling that I've been talking to Ray Kroc, the founder of McDonald's, just as he began to expand. I ask Steve Poses if he worries about, or enjoys, taking risks.

"Oh sure," he smiles. "Both. But it's incremental. It's like . . . like a relationship. It's not a bolt of lightning. For me, at least. There may be some people who suddenly commit themselves. Involvement at first sight. But for most of us, you take a little risk. That works out. So you take another and see how that works. That works. You take another. Pretty soon, there you are—living together, buying a house to rehab together, married, whatever. It's incremental. I think business is like that. I take little risks, and then other little risks, and then five years later people look at the incremental results and say, 'Wow, what a risk taker!' Actually—things just follow."

An hour later we're riding out from center-city Philadelphia to my alma mater, to the University of Pennsylvania campus in the western part of the city.

"If you haven't been back to school since the sixties, you'll find the mood of this place different," says Steve. "You know, our restaurants are products of the sixties, as I said. But it's more than that. The people who work in the front of the house —the waiters and waitresses and bartenders and food servers —are in some ways frustrated because they're not doing something else. They're in transition. Some of them have been in transition for years now. Since we opened. We have a lot of painters, a lot of writers. Aspiring for eight years now. The restaurant is a good place to aspire in. It affords a lifestyle where you can continue to pursue your art—and still make a living, a very good living.

"Maybe the restaurant is also a way of postponing the knowledge that you're never going to be the world's greatest writer or artist. Sometimes that catches up to people. We have people on our staff who've been with us a long time, and sometimes they aren't as good to the customers as we'd like. What do you do about that? You keep them on. You talk to them. We have a responsibility to our people. I know you, as a restaurant critic, are going to say that you, and everyone else has a right to good service. We have a responsibility to our customers too—we know that. But we keep people on. You just talk to them, tell them that just because they're having career problems with their art, that doesn't mean they should take the frustration out on the customer. Actually, what we do is work therapy with them.

"But even with the frustrations, the fact that we had artists and writers on staff made things more interesting. It gave a texture and richness to the front of the house. Our staff and our customers were essentially the same people, from the same backgrounds.

Our restaurants are popular with people eating alone, and that's partly why. You know that singles are always supposed to be trouble in a restaurant—the waiter makes the same number of trips, but there's an empty seat at the table and an empty space on the bill. Nobody ever stops to figure that the time might come when you have nobody to sit at that table—because you've discouraged all the singles. But our staff helps by being our staff—if you come in alone, they keep you company. Or they seem to.

"Anyway, in the eighties, my guess is that these new kids are not going to have that luxury—they're not going to be able to afford postponing their careers for a few years while they hang out and earn money in a restaurant. You know, after Charles Reich's *The Greening of America* appeared—in 1970, I think —Peter Drucker wrote an article—I forget where—called 'The Bluing of America'—America getting on its work clothes. His point was that the greening was only going to be a transition, a period of a few years until the competition for jobs took over. And even he didn't deal with the economy of scarcity we're going toward now. We could experiment back then. We had all those years to make mistakes in. This generation is going to have to start from the beginning competing for the fewer and fewer jobs that become available. Of course, as a businessman, I know I can get lots of very eager workers. Willing to learn. Attentive. As a restaurant owner, though, I know that my business depends on that creativity, that willingness to experiment . . . on not being afraid of the small risks that add up to big ones."

International House looms above us like a white fortress now. Vaguely reminiscent of Indian cliff dwellings or Tibetan monasteries, it is a huge skyscraper of raw concrete honeycombed with identical windows—as impersonal and cold and inhuman as modern architecture is capable of being. We walk along a deserted cement patio, with its little cement Stonehenge of modernistic benches, toward the sheets of glass that make up the first floor. We push through plain modern glass doors and are in another world.

The light is dim and warm. The floor is warm orange quarry tile, and to the right of the entry is the dark bar made of quarry tile, with big blocks of glass brick lit from behind. There are tables around the bar and a huge island of quarry tile filled with green plants and trees and actual flowers.

"It doesn't look like fast food," I say, "with all those plants."

"Well, we had the window wall here and it faced south . . . All the high-sunlight plants are on the window side. We figure they'll all die—you have to figure that with all plants in a restaurant—but we think we can retard the process at a rate where we can afford replacements. There's going to be a waterfall—just a little three-foot spill really—behind the bar. It looks nice, and it sounds nice. Sound is an element of restaurant decor that is relatively easy to control and nobody bothers with it.

"Over here is the cafeteria line. We have hamburgers, vegetarian hamburgers—that's new for the student market—and chili. That's new too. Our hamburgers are six-ounce burgers— two more than a quarter pounder. They come with roast potatoes—we don't deep fry potatoes because we don't deep fry anything. And they have a little bit of alfalfa sprout on top.

Which tastes good and which reminds you that this is a different kind of fast food.

"Our burgers are thick and come rare, medium or well. Fast-food burgers—I should say other fast-food burgers—are thin so they can be cooked fast and then kept hot under a lamp. We need to get a jump on our burgers, so we always have some on the grill. The chef starts them rare and then moves them when they become medium and well . . . We have a very tight control on how long the burgers are kept—because we don't throw them away when they get to be well done. We put them in the chili. That's the purpose of the chili on the menu.

"For six ounces of choice beef—no organs or offal—we charge three-fifty, with the roast potatoes. McDonald's costs less, but for less meat in a plastic-foam container that first of all reminds you that you're eating fast food, and, second, steams everything soft.

"We have a wine-of-the-day at nine-fifty a bottle—a Spanish cabernet sauvignon that costs over five dollars retail—and you can get a big glass of it for two-fifty. We sell a lot of wine. We change the wine-of-the-day every day—Commissary can supply this place with over seventy-five different wines—and we have a California jug wine at around a dollar a glass.

"Frank Donnelly is the man in charge of both Edens. Two years ago he was a swimming coach and a manager of a tennis club. He was thirty-five years old. He didn't see too much of a future for himself in that. Somebody he knew that I knew suggested he might like to be a restaurant entrepreneur. We put him through the Commissary for a year, and now he's our Eden manager. And he's great. You know, I always say it's easy to open restaurants—what's hard is keeping them good. It's like a basketball team. All teams are enthusiastic for the first few games. It's when you have to get up for that seventieth game that you begin to see the difference in teams. And that's what Frank is good at—he sees this like a competition, which it is—like a performance, which it is. And he coaches the team. He does a terrific job getting these kids up for the struggle. And that's what it is, a struggle."

Students and faculty move through the line at Eden. Other

students on the other side of the line serve them—some with a kind of awe that says "Here I am, actually making food that's better than anything I've ever tasted before." Others already have that air of self-satisfied and self-congratulatory competence which is the special public attitude of very good and very young waiters.

"The people are really very good," says Steve Poses. "And you know, this doesn't take any imagination. It isn't hard. It doesn't cost us anything to have a wine-of-the-day. We're going to start a coffee-of-the-day. Different flavors, different blends. In the spring we'll take that empty plaza and fill it with tables, and increase our seating from two hundred to two hundred fifty or three hundred. Some plants. Some color . . ."

We're walking out the door and across the plaza on a cold February night, and I tell Steve that he sounds as if he's a little restless. As if it's all become too easy.

"Oh," he laughs. "You should see our new place—the Market. It's a convenience store—for people who care about their conveniences. Homemade pasta you can buy fresh or frozen and take home and cook in minutes. Sauces to go on top of it. Cheeses. Pâtés. You only have to look at the demographics. More and more families among professionals are families where two people are working. People who get tired of cooking when they come home after a ten- or sometimes twelve-hour day. People who are sick of eating out all the time. Now they can have the same good food—prepared by people who care about food—with no trouble and for a lot less money. Like Commissary and Eden, there's a fifteen percent discount to begin with because you don't tip—and we don't need skilled workers to dispense food that the customer is going to cook or reheat. We've worked very hard *not* to make the Market into a gourmet store—we want it to be a convenience store.

"Convenience stores have grown much faster than fast-food shops in the past three years—the Seven-Eleven stores and places like that. But, once again, they're not providing the food that the upper middle class is used to. So we have home-baked breads you can buy, fresh salads, fresh seafood. We're doing very well. We'll do better."

"I'm as positive about the Market as I can be about anything. Except"—Steve turns as we're about to get in the car for the ride back to center city—"except the only problem may be demographics. History. The women's movement was really made possible by expanding employment opportunities. When women came into the job market in large numbers, they found discrimination and they found that they needed support organizations to defend them. In an economy of scarcity, 'last in, first out' will start to operate. Men have power and they'll attempt to assert that power. The economy itself poses a lot of problems for the women's movement. And that means serious implications"—he smiles broadly and gets into the car—"for my takeout food store. That's what I tell people when they ask me why I'm still around, supporting those old sixties causes that a lot of them got tired of. Peace. Women's rights. Jobs. I tell them they're all important to my business. *Necessary* to my business."

That sounds, I say, as if you're doing something like rationalizing again—defining your business in a way that lets you do what you think would be a lot of fun to do anyway.

"Oh sure," Steve says, laughing, as we drive away from the his shiny Eden, glowing out from its concrete framework. "Sure. My business is taking risks."

EIGHT

SMILES OF A SUMMER NIGHT

"Cheese with. You know what I think, I think Marie's trying to get Michael back."

"Well, I got something to tell you then. Cheese without. Marie can have him. The last time I saw Michael was three hours ago and he was already drunk and plus eating a ice cream cone and plus up in Chinatown waiting in line to get another tattoo."

If there was a song that went "I wish they all could be South Philly girls," they'd be on the album cover. Kelly has a golden forehead band rucked under the crimped folds of her blond hair and wears a shining silver top that might be and probably is the visible half of a one-piece bathing suit, and a pair of short shorts, blue and white in alternating three-inch stripes, that button demurely and fascinatingly around her thighs and puff out wide, like the doublet part of medieval doublet and hose. Rita has dark-gleaming black hair that hangs to her waist and wears a pale-pink dress with a bright red rose on its hip and lace eyelets running down not quite revealingly across her breasts. It is the newest and most stylish dress of the night, the new mid-thigh neo-mini, and it looks a child's ball gown on a not quite fully grown woman, who is growing before your eyes.

"Extra cheese with," says the tired man, who will say very little else. Bagged dungarees, the belt sagging down under his heavy stomach, a no-color no-designer T-shirt with a breast pocket that holds a comb and a pack of regular-length nonfilter cigarettes. He has no hair to his ears, then a heavy dark mane that still sweeps neatly to the ghost of a D.A. in back. He yawns—benignly, cheerlessly, resolutely and thoroughly drunk. Drunk as an accomplishment, the accomplishment of a hard worker who gets drunk once a week.

"The ladies of South Philly will have a quiet table in a dark corner so their mascara will shine. For the solitary yawning gentleman, something solid on which to lean. The three *garçons* behind us will have another round of drinks—perhaps in three years, when they are of legal age," or something like that, says the French maître d' of one of Philadelphia's best French restaurants to the French waiter from another restaurant, in French, so the ladies and the yawning man never give him a look. *"Fromage avec,"* he says to the register man, who gives him a cheese with.

"Cheese mushroom with and extracheese extramushroom with and extrameat extracheese extramushroom with." Three young men in the same dungaree shorts, high white socks, running shoes and T-shirts. The first T-shirt is rolled up to expose a dark, hard, tanned stomach; the second has been cut off right under the owner's nipples; the third hangs down outside the shorts, stretching almost to cover them. They are sixteen, and they are not at all drunk. But they can't help acting drunk. This is Pat's Steaks. Saturday night. Three A.M.

"This is Pat's Steaks," says Frank Olivieri, owner and general manager. "Pat's King of Steaks. Somebody shoots a President, the reporters are down here. The Eagles are winning. The Phillies are losing. The reporters are down here again. You want to know what the man in the street thinks about something—this is where you come to ask him."

Frank is tanned and muscular, bearded and friendly. He likes to talk about his steaks and he tells the story of the invention of the steak sandwich with the easy, practiced air of a man who has done it many times before.

"My father, Harry, and my uncle, Pat, had a stand down here in the 1920s, selling hot dogs a nickel each. Well, you get awful tired eating hot dogs and instead they'd go over a store on the corner, buy themselves a loaf of Italian bread, some steaks, slice it up and fry it for themselves. When they were alone. You don't like people to see you not eating your own hot dogs. When you sell hot dogs. So when a customer catches them, they say, what's that? And they let on like it's a new item on the menu they're testing. Gimme one, says the customer, and then they come back and ask for them—pretty soon they forgot all about the hot dog business and did nothing but steaks.

"I started here when I was eleven years old. I'd sell watermelon and corn on the cob out front. My father'd give me five bucks, I'd take the bus up Woodside Park. You remember that old amusement park? Gone for years now . . . And when I finished school my father wanted me to go to college. I had the marks, I was accepted. I was going to Penn State . . . I told my father, I don't want to go. He's disappointed. But I said, face it, I'm going to wind up here anyway, and going to school I'm just losing four years . . . of money. So I took over this business when I was eighteen. My father and uncle retired, and I ran it. A kid eighteen years old telling men how they're supposed to do their job. It was hard. But that was the way it had to be. And that was the way it was. I'm still never more than an hour away, I live in Packer Park, I got a summer home down in Brigantine, New Jersey. I can be here any time, and I am here lots and lots of the time. I like it. You get to meet a lot of people. People don't know I'm the owner—do I look like an owner? But they know I work at Pat's, and they know me. Lots of famous people come in here—Jack Klugman, David Brenner, the Bee Gees, Jackson Five . . . you name a big act around here, they come to Pat's. Sylvester Stallone did part of *Rocky* here, a nice guy. He calls and invites me a private party after, I have to tell him I can't go. Why not, he says. Why not? I'm working, I say. You're hard, he says. Hard, I say, we didn't get to be number one by letting the business run itself.

"You know, the business has to come first. I remember once there was a contest for the best cheese steak in Philly. I didn't enter. I have a business to run—I can't go entering contests. So the winner of the best steak in Philadelphia—without counting Pat's yes or no—gets a free trip to Chicago for three days and goes on television there. Some reporter from a paper calls me up and asks me what I think about this. Great, I say. He says aren't you upset you didn't get a chance to go to Chicago? Chicago? I say, I can't even get the time to drive an hour away down in Brigantine and you want me to go to Chicago? For three days?

"People don't think. Here's Bloomingdale's department store in New York, they want me to come up for a week—a week!—and make cheese steaks and sell them in some kind of festival they got. I say you must be crazy. First of all I got my best men here, I got my grill here, I got my own business here. You want me to leave my business alone and go up and build up your business? Take my best men? Or leave my men and have somebody up there cooking god knows what and calling it Pat's Steaks? This is our only location. A Pat's Steak is cooked at Pat's.

"And I like it. If I don't like it, I don't sell it. I get all my bread from the same bakery, the same bakery that's been supplying my father and uncle since back when they used to sneak across to the grocery and buy it on the sly. I get my meat from different suppliers—but before it comes in, I get it, I slice it up and cook it up and eat it. If it doesn't eat right, it doesn't go out to the customers.

"And that's why you'll never see an ad for Pat's Steaks. Our customers are our ads. Famous customers—David Brenner—he talks about us on TV. You know what it would cost you to have Johnny Carson mention your product on TV? You can't buy that. But Johnny Carson mentions Pat's Steaks. And the regular customer, the guy who's not on TV, he mentions Pat's Steaks. So our steaks have to be right. No portion control. We use eyeroll beef only. No cheap rolls, Vilotti & Marinelli Bakery. Good onions that we chop by hand. Nothing that we can't make the best. People ask me, why don't you have onion rings. I say, you want onion rings, go to McDonald's. Why don't you have veal scaloppine? You want veal scaloppine, you have to go somewhere else. We got what we got—and it's good. Ironically, now. I spent my life working here. We got guys who go back forty years. If you count when I started, I got thirty-two years. My son, Frankie, just graduated from Friend's Select School, ready to go on to Penn State—he's not going to college. He says no, he's going to PSU—Pat's Steaks University, and he's already working on the grill."

"Two cheese . . . um, without? And extracheese . . . um, with? Did I do it right?" she giggles. "I did it right! The first time I ever ordered!"

A summer night, breathing air that feels like it's oozed through a wet sponge, dense air that seems to cuddle up in your crotch and armpits like a wet animal. Air that sweats on you. Two tall, thin Black women, clouds of talcum visible across their chests and necks inside white summer sundresses. They touch heads when they giggle, and they giggle often with the gray-haired Black man behind them. He has a neatly trimmed, curly gray beard and a neatly pressed pearly gray suit, white shirt, maroon tie, white felt hat with matching maroon band, highly polished black shoes and high maroon socks that are entirely visible because the pants to his suit are walking shorts and reach only to his knees. Behind them, a short sullen-looking white guy with red hair, blunt pale face, and red, sore-looking eyes. "Cheese without," he grumbles, in a voice that probably always grumbles, and walks quickly back to his small panel truck, white, with the name of the company that used to own it blotched out with big smears of purple paint. The hood of the truck is open, and cables run from its battery to the battery of a maroon Buick that still looks almost sleek and new, though it's seven or eight years old.

"I want to thank you," says the Black guy in the short pants suit. "This muh is getting old on me. And I want to pay you."

"Helping people is what it's all about," grumbles the grumbler, shaking his head. "I'm happy to do it."

The women slip into the front seat. Music fills the muggy air, something that sounds at once electronically generated, sentimental and rhythmic, over a disco beat. The Black guy keeps waving a bill at the white man—unsuccessfully. Finally he says, "But how about another?"

"I never turn down another cheese steak," the white guy actually smiles as he grumbles, and the two of them get back on line together.

"It jumps here at night," says Lenny Zappala, night manager of Pat's for fifteen years. He wears a white T-shirt, an apron, a big gold watch and ring. The cheerful, easygoing kind of manager, the kind that workers like, and that gets more work out of workers than any other kind. "I started here when I was twelve, after school, I worked in other places. I had my own business for a while . . . I come back to Pat's . . . It's my line of work. It's . . . bananas. This is a night business here. I mean, days they busy, but nights . . . we start picking up around eleven-thirty, with the movie crowd, then if there's a game—baseball, football, we get that crowd. Two o'clock the bars close, we get a rush. Four o'clock the clubs close, we get a rush. Five o'clock Jersey closes, we get another rush. After that we get the club bartenders. Then . . . you start all over again with the morning workers. It's nothing to see a guy in a tux, leaning on his Mercedes or Seville or something and another guy in work clothes, a bricklayer or carpenter maybe, leaning on *his* Mercedes or Seville, because they make a good buck. One's been out all night, one's just getting up in the morning, both of them want a cheese steak to make them feel less tired. We see everything. We see . . . four five times a year, they come up naked and say, 'Cheese with.' College kids, I figure, maybe a fraternity or two has the pledges come down and get a cheese steak naked? Maybe a sorority, too, because we get that once in a while."

"What do you do when a woman comes up naked and asks for a cheese with?" I say.

"What do we do? Give her a cheese with and say, 'Next.' And give the next whatever it is whatever it wants. You think you're going to make Pat's Steaks fall down and faint if you take your clothes off? We see it all here. Those sheets—couple of years ago, we'd get four or five toga parties a week. That's dying out now. Nice kids, college kids. We get them now. We get more in the fall. Exam times, we can tell—they come later, they look tired. Sometimes with crazy makeup, gorilla masks, Nixon faces, Reagan faces—with a sign that says PAT'S HOT SAUCE IS A VEGETABLE, Coneheads, Star Wars . . . They get along here. Everybody gets along. No fights, no trouble. We give them a sandwich fast, they get the sandwich they don't have anything else to talk about. They get another sandwich. Or they leave. Where you going to hang around here? And we treat everybody the same. No reservations. No special service. You're a millionaire, or you just got the price of a steak together by digging up all the money in your pockets—and we get plenty of both—you're equal at Pat's. Black or white or anything else. You're a customer. We get our regulars. Keep coming back year after year. I watch them grow up, go to college, become doctors and lawyers. They still come back. And I'm still here. Professor of Cheese Steaks."

It's a fact we all know but never mention that pay phones are only used for two things. Saying "I love you" to people we don't live with and saying "Of course I still love you, I'll just be a little late, that's all" to people we do live with. That is what is going on right now, on the frequently used pay phone right by the soda window at Pat's Steak. The woman is in her late twenties, in a soft-blue wraparound dress that has a little gold edge all around the neckline, the sleeves, the hem and the wraparound part of the skirt that falls open as she shifts from foot to foot, exposing long legs in thin, gauze-white stockings. "But Harry . . . But Harry . . . ," she says every half minute or so, making faces back over her shoulder at her friend. "But Harry, your sister's right here. I'll put her on."

Harry's sister, in bright purple knickers, shoes that seem to be nothing but three-inch heels, silky purple strings, and just enough sole to hold them all together, has a blue blouse whose sleeves fall over her arms in pale, translucent waves. She has to struggle to push a sleeve back and see her watch.

"Harry . . . I know . . . It's four o'clock about," says Harry's sister. "O.K., almost five. There was an office party. We had a couple drinks. You ever have a couple drinks? Or did you quit yesterday? So we might've had a couple extra drinks. And we decided—yes, for no reason—to drive across the Walt Whitman Bridge to Pat's for a steak. We'll be back . . . No, not in five minutes! In a couple hours . . . stop being stupid now. We're not falling-down drunk. I'm driving, not Ellen. I can drive. Harry . . . this is your sister. I'm not going to let anything happen. It's O.K., O.K.?"

She hangs up with a smile and turns to fold herself into the arms of a big blond guy behind her. He has slicked-down hair that is just starting to stand up out of its slicks, because he hasn't combed it for hours, and he's just starting to sober up and just starting to realize—with the expression of a man who's been given a wonderful gift and doesn't know why—that he's scored.

"You and Joe are all right," she giggles across to where Ellen is folded into her own date's arms. "Now you got to call up Fred for me. You want another one? Cheese without?"

"You want another one? You hear that all the time outside," says Charles Compagnucci, day manager at Pat's. He is a big broad-shouldered man with a big neat beard. "And you know why you hear that? Because of the bread. We use Italian bread, but we use a French-loaf-style Italian bread. It doesn't fill you up. You get plenty of meat, plenty of cheese and onions. And you still have room if you feel like another. That's a trade secret. But we don't need trade secrets—our secret is—we're Pat's Steaks.

"I'm the day manager, I know how this place works. I could go get a place of my own, do all the same things. So what? It wouldn't be Pat's. I wouldn't have the location. I wouldn't have the reputation. I wouldn't have the turnover. It wouldn't be as safe. It couldn't be. Where else can a couple girls walk up, three or four in the morning, and eat and nobody bothers them? You can't walk on South Street after two. Center city? You'd be crazy. *I* wouldn't walk there. This place is safer because it doesn't have any place to eat but just standing outside, where you buy your steak. You don't have to worry about going out on the street—because Pat's is the street. No parking lot muggings—we got no parking lot. We have a police station right around the corner on Eleventh Street, and we have a lot of cops who are customers—plainclothes, detectives, narcs. Frank always says he knew every narc in the city by the time he was fifteen. If there are twenty people outside, one of them is a cop. We get a guy looks at somebody else's girl once in a while, but that's over before it starts—no place is as safe as Pat's.

"And you can't get a fresher sandwich. We get our bread every day. The old loaves we just throw out. That sounds like we're wasting money, but if you saw the difference between day-old loaves and fresh loaves—you'd throw it out too. We have one guy, his job ten hours a day is cutting bread. Nothing else."

Compagnucci leads me over to a big stainless-steel restaurant table. On it is a big metal saw, its blade in a steel housing, with a steel chute down the side. "This is where we slice the loaf. The bread just gets fed into this chute and the saw slits it in half. The blade is as clean as any knife, and much faster. We don't have time to slit by hand. We cut the loaf into sandwich rolls by hand though." Compagnucci shows me an inch-thick professional cutting board. Deep grooves are worn in it. "You put the bread here, you slice here and here—once in a while somebody says they get a short sandwich, once in a very great while. I wish I could show them this. Those grooves get worn in from the knife coming down again and again in the same place. We get a new cutting board every two, three months. We have a slicer over here, a supermarket slicer, and we cut all our own meat. It comes out of the freezer just under freezing temperature because that way it's easiest to cut. We move our steaks so fast we can do that. Anybody else that tries, without our volume, the meat would spoil on them. We have a guy does nothing else ten hours a day but slice meat. Upstairs, come on I'll show you." We walk upstairs to where Kevin Manuel is chopping onions. He fits each big number-one onion in a commercial slicer set right over a big tub and pulls the lever. It takes five or six seconds to chop an onion.

"Ten hours a day, seven days a week, we have a man who does nothing but chop onions," says Compagnucci. "You get fresh bread, fresh meat, fresh onions at Pat's. Now come downstairs, and walk right in the grill room."

A small triangular room, the grill takes up three quarters of its longest wall. There is a small pile of meat in the corner, and a man putting new steaks on the middle of the grill. At the register is Nick Caccio, sixty-six, who has worked at Pat's Steaks for forty years.

Compagnucci explains how the kitchen works. Nick is the register man. He says "Next?" and repeats the customer's order. The cheese man stands next to Nick. He repeats the order again, and hands the makeup man the bread. The makeup man opens in the bread, in one quick movement, against his apron, and scoops up pieces of meat from the little pile of already cooked steak. He hands it to the cheese man who, more often than not, puts on a big smear of melted Kraft Cheez Whiz and then gives the sandwich to the customer, who has already paid Nick. It takes less time to do all this than it took you to read about it.

"We try to keep four or five sandwiches up, and we figure we make a sandwich in eight seconds," says Compagnucci. "Cheese steaks are fast food—and Pat's is the fastest. I don't care where you go, which kind of place. You take ten people to a McDonald's, for example, and you take ten people to Pat's Steaks. Some of those people are going to be on line in McDonald's fifteen, twenty, thirty minutes later. Here, they got to be gone in five minutes. So you get a fresh sandwich, a fast sandwich. We don't have sandwiches sitting on the grill in grease—they move on and off in two minutes. The grill man sees they're slowing down, he puts on less, that's his responsibility. The makeup man, he's responsible for the sandwich— we tell him what we want. But this isn't portion control and every piece of meat on this grill is different. It's his judgment of what a sandwich is. He can't put on too much meat or he hurts the business. He can't put on too little meat or he hurts the customer and that hurts the business even more. So we need good grill men, and we need good makeup men. You're taking bread, you can't look at it to see where the cut is, you have to know by feel where the cut is. You watch the makeup man he's looking at the meat, he's turning the bread, opening it flat, flipping the meat in to lay flat, seeing there's no bare spots in the sandwich which we never want, scooping onions . . . Experienced men, twenty years or so, they come in here, they're greenhorns. I was on the grill myself and it took six months before I got the motions down. So another one of our trade secrets is we keep our people. Good salaries, good benefits, good working conditions. We close four days a year now. That's something that started now, when the sons and grandsons took over. It's hard to work the big holidays. We close Christmas, New Year's, Thanksgiving and Easter. You know, the funny thing is—when we decided to close, we didn't know how. This building had never been closed up. There were no windows for the space over the grill. First we used plywood. Now finally we got custom made windows we can close.

"Finally, our biggest trade secret—this is Pat's Steaks," says Compagnucci. "A customer gets a steak here—the ingredients are fresh, they get it fast. Our people are happy workers—not like those underpaid high school kids you see in the hamburger places . . . Even more than all that, the customer puts that steak in his mouth, he knows it's a Pat's Steak. We have the psychological advantage. That's important, and I'll tell you something that shows you how important. Though you'll think I'm kidding you. I work here, I eat these steaks. They're good steaks. We all eat them. Things slow down a little, nothing goes to waste by sitting on that grill longer than two minutes. On my day off, I come by sometimes and get myself a steak and—you know why?—they taste better outside! Not just a little bit better—good as they are in here—they taste great, when they're somebody else's job."

"I was in at the Yard during the war," says Nick Caccio. "The Navy Yard, in World War II. And I helped out here, and then got out of the Yard, and I thought I'd give this place a try. I didn't think it'd be permanent, but it turned out to be"— Nick pauses, telling what is almost a family joke at Pat's—"so far, anyway. I live just down the street . . . in the house with the clean steps . . . and this is a good job, good money, you get to meet a lot of people . . ."

Nick tells me about the grill. It is made of half-inch armor plate, a special extra-hard steel, and wears out, with the cleaning, every eight or ten years. "When we get a new one, it's flat, and we want it to have a dent in it so the oil runs off the back of the grill, so we have to heat it up and then pound it with a sledgehammer till it bends. They make them up special for us. Nothing we use is just ordinary."

"How old do you think I am?" says Louis Vilotti, of Vilotti & Marinelli Bakery.

"Fifty, fifty-five," I say.

"I'm sixty-six, and you know what this is?" He waves a jar of dark brown-red stuff at me. "This is Pat's hot sauce. A family secret I been eating since I started supplying bread to them. I get this to take home with me. I put it on steaks. I put it on sausage. I give it to the wife to cook with. It burns out the germs. It burns out the cancer. It kept me healthy. I got all my teeth. I want you to put, right in that article, I got all my teeth because of Pat's hot sauce."

Compagnucci has another reason to like Pat's hot sauce. "We don't get many people at night who aren't a little ripped. Or with the munchies. I mean, what are you doing out at four A.M. if you haven't been partying. We're used to them—we like them. This is like a party. One good thing about Pat's hot sauce, though—it sobers you up. And gives you enough to think about to keep you busy. Until you're ready to say, You want another?"

"You want another?"

"No, but you ga'head," says the girl, her face pale in the beginning blue of the morning sky. She is short, freckled, and with pale orange-red hair. She lets the large teenage boy lean over her and tend her, running a proprietary finger now and then down her bare arm. She looks cool, quiet and pleased. He is a little drunk still, even after all the hot sauce he put on the first cheese-with, but he smiles around a big mouthful of his second, sucking in air to cool his tongue, and turns his arm toward her proudly to show off a big raw brand-new tattoo of a melting ice cream cone. Michael's back—and Marie's got him once again.

NINE

WHY IT TASTES SO BAD

Here is a traditional recipe from an aristocratic old New York hotel, famous for its banquets:

> Take a griddle and heat it to 800°. Take several hundred three-inch-thick filet mignons and sear them black, one minute a side. This will seal in the juices and prevent them from drying out entirely. Then pop them in a slow oven (200°) for two hours. At the end of that time you will have an odd little piece of meat, part-grilled, part-roasted, part-steam-tabled, which will look like an ordinary filet broiled to a passable medium. Call it either medium-rare or medium, according to the customer's order, and call the last ones out of the oven well done. Serve with every possible flourish—a scrap of watercress, a mushroom cap, a puddle of canned beef gravy —and charge at least five dollars more than the highest priced steak house in town.
>
> The filet will be tasteless from all the slow cooking, and at best lukewarm (a temperature at which, since it's neither hot nor cold, we should, according to Jesus Christ, vomit from our mouths). And there may be a little trouble with people who order their filet rare—instruct your waiters to say, with all the aristocratic old haute-cuisine hauteur they can muster, "The chef will not serve our filet mignon overrare. The meat

must, after all, be cooked to be properly enjoyed." Something like that should overawe any malcontents.

The old filet recipe represents the triumph of Modern Restaurant Management in the 1960s. Rather than paying a chef to stand around and cook, Modern Management used a short-order cook—the tradition in this famous hotel was that he got two quarts of beer, free, to replace the water he lost in sweat standing over the griddle. And the filet itself became something a waiter could take from an oven, decorate, and serve—without talking to anyone in the kitchen. And with no danger of burning his fingers.

Now here is another recipe, assembled from *Restaurant Business,* the magazine of Modern Restaurant Management, in 1981:

> *Buy prefrozen, boneless, portion-controlled prime rib, presliced, prebrowned around the edges, already roasted a uniform rare. Slice, plate, cover with vented polyfilm and cook sixty seconds on high in a microwave. Serve it a perfect medium rare with Skincredible Shells, frozen prebrowned potato skin "with just enough potato left on" to form them into identical little scoops. Skincredibles will heat right along with the rib, and can be lavished with sour-cream-type filling or, for a nouvelle cuisine touch, frozen avocado pulp . . .*

It's easy to make fun of prefrozen *haute cuisine* and imitation ingredients—and that's exactly what I'm going to do. But first I should point out that 1981 prime rib, although it is not prime, and has probably come from some part of a steer that is nowhere near the rib, definitely tastes better than the 1960s filet did. The purpose of Modern Restaurant Management, however, has not changed. The chef has been replaced by an unskilled employee, who now does not even have to know how to use a flipper and who no longer requires two quarts of beer as a prize; the waiter can still pick up the plate without burning his fingers (microwaves heat only the food), and the only conversation necessary in the kitchen should be about whose job it is to take off that sheet of vented polyfilm.

The prime rib has not been treated well—but it has been

treated better. It is not as dry as the filet, it has actually been roasted once upon a time, and it has some real food value left in it. Microwaves have, in fact, improved mediocre food all across America—and I hope, for the sake of the banquet customers, that the aristocratic old New York hotel has switched over from the old-fashion beer and griddles of the past to the fake-food wizardry of the future.

It is enlightening to read magazines like *Restaurant Business* and *Quick Frozen Foods International*—two of the many publications directed at restaurant middle managers. You know the kind of people I mean—hardworking, troubled, ambitious, determined to be understanding (the better to manipulate employees and customers), friendly, resolute, and utterly untrustworthy. The kind of people who run America.

You need a little glossary of terms to understand all of *RB* and *QFFI*. IQF, for example, means "individually quick frozen," usually an entree, complete with sauce, that comes in its own polyfilm bag and can be "plated" (slid onto a plate in one icy chunk) in a trice, microwaved by an unskilled worker, and "menued" (listed on the menu with a fanciful description). Knorr-Swiss, a company that makes many different canned and dried sauces and soups, advertises that its instant mousse powder "can be menued at ten times food cost." High praise, but not the highest. Makers of iced-tea mix, that oddly powdery drink you find in more and more diners and cafeterias, advertise that it costs "less than two cents per serving." Remember that, the next time you find it menued at seventy-five cents—thirty-seven and a half times food cost.

An attractive IQF entree should have "good plate coverage." Fish and extended-meat manufacturers always wax ecstatic about the plate coverage of their products. So do the manufacturers of funny-looking shapes of french fries. "Plate appeal" means it looks good on the plate—subtly different from plate coverage; Alaskan king-crab claws, which are delivered precooked and frozen anywhere you eat them outside Alaska, usually claim "higher plate appeal" than shrimp or lobster, because three or four of these fibrous limbs can be piled crisscrossed on a plate, like a half-hearted attempt at campfire building, and made to look like more than they are.

"Mouth feel," another important term, is always described as "natural"—which means that when you put a cube of imitation meat or cheese in your mouth it doesn't seem as if you're biting down on a wad of cellophane or a spoonful of Crisco. Frequently mouth feel is called "improved natural mouth feel" —a confession from the fashioners of the stuff that they were exaggerating a little when they claimed natural mouth feel for their creations in the past.

French fries are the single most competitive and highly advertised item in restaurant magazines. There are, of course, no french fries in American restaurants. To make french fries, you peel a potato, cut it into small shapes, and deep fry it. To make what are called french fries in an American restaurant, you need a processor, who cuts the potato into tiny shapes, frequently leaves the skin on to give it "improved plate appeal," and then processes it—dehydrates and precooks it at the same time. French fries have almost completely replaced baked potatoes in mediocre restaurants—and I'll let a french-fry processor tell you why:

"ORDINARY; EXTRAORDINARY," trumpets a double-page, four-color ad comparing baked potatoes with Simplot Ranch Cuts. Baked potatoes:

> *Are ordinary . . .*
> *Raw costs are up and climbing . . .*
> *Good bakers are hard to find.*
> *But that's only the beginning.*
> *You have to scrub and oil them. Waste lots of oven room and energy baking and holding them. Wrap them in foil and serve them with plenty of butter and sour cream.*
> *And you can't predict demand; at the end of the night you're either running out or throwing out.*

But extraordinary Simplot Ranch Cuts:

> *Are different . . .*
> *Hearty slices of potato with skin still on . . .*
> *Don't need to be served with butter and sour cream . . .*

Cut out guesswork and waste.
Six plate filling ounces are reasonably priced, including oil, labor and energy. . . .

What middle manager cannot see the value in Ranch Cuts? And if you don't like Ranch Cuts, you can have almost any shape you want—french fries with only a tip of skin left on, french fries concertina-shaped, or "crinkle cut," french fries shaped like huge potato chips with the skin on. Ore-Ida calls them "Potato Planks" and praises their improved plate coverage. Ore-Ida also guarantees of its frozen steak fries that "50% are over 3 inches and a maximum of 7% under 2 inches." Larger fries take up more room and look better: increased plate coverage and plate appeal "for a lower cost per serving."

Many makers warn against "bargain" fries (their quotation marks). Bargain fries, it turns out, are underprocessed. Devious manufacturers have not sufficiently precooked them, to save on their own energy bills. "Bargain" fries are "often shipped practically raw . . . short on servings, long on water," more like real potatoes, in short. "Waterlogged, underprocessed fries take longer to cook . . . the excess water you cook out can make your oil break down faster, turn rancid, discolor," and you have to change it from time to time, increasing costs. Frymax, a frying oil, advertises that normal oil breaks down after a mere 2,734 ten-ounce servings of chicken and four-ounce servings of french fries have been fried in it, while Frymax, abnormal in a way that is not revealed, does not break down until 2,948 servings have been fried.

I sometimes have the feeling that I've been unlucky enough to receive the 2,947th Frymaxed chicken—dark flecks in the artfully induced nooks and crannies of the breading, and tasting as if it had been marinated for a week in sour chicken soup.

But back to potatoes. Shoestring potatoes, and potatoes cut so thin they should be called noodle potatoes, are more and more popular in fast-food chains. Here's the reason: the thinner they are, the more servings management gets. "5.2 regular servings a pound vs. 4 regular competitive servings," says an ad for Farm Fries Shoestrings. Plus, shoestrings cook in 120 seconds at 335° Fahrenheit, vs. 180 seconds at 350° for regular fries. Turn down the heat, speed up the serving line, increase servings—buy these shreds of desiccated precooked potato and make more money out of everybody who orders them.

Of course, baked potatoes are still possible in a restaurant with a really clever middle manager. Here is a recipe paraphrased from *RB:*

> *For baked potato. Put medium potatoes (eighty to ninety count per fifty lb.) in a microwave one inch apart. High heat ten to fourteen minutes. Let stand three minutes* [possibly so that they will be easy to handle, but *RB* doesn't say why]. *Slice the top off, remove pulp, mix it with any dressing* [*RB* recommends chili sauce, another nouvelle-cuisine touch], *restuff, and refrigerate. Reheat to order in two minutes. Only 120 seconds, quick as a shoestring fry.*

Breaded food is the second most popular item in restaurant magazines. "Japanese breading" is a new process, whereby tiny flakes, which appear to be chips of breadcrust, are made to adhere to fish or flesh. The thick and ragged nature of the coating has lots of plate appeal and increased plate coverage, but up until the middle of 1981, there was a problem—some of the stuff used to drop off, baring the food underneath, and resulting in "lowered customer appeal." But *QFFI* happily reports that a new process has eliminated that defect; now improved Japanese breading is available in "natural and artificial colors . . . including natural, white, toasted, lemon, peach, caramel, orange, and dark yellow." It may come as a shock to some patrons of fast-food stands, but the appetizing color of deep-fried chicken and fish is not from frying but from the dye in the breading.

Pierce Oven-Wing-Dings are especially designed for the manager with only half a kitchen: even if you don't have a deep fryer you can serve these precooked, prebrowned wings. They "heat up crunchy on the outside" with a few minutes in either conventional or microwave oven. Treasure Isle, a seafood processor, offers Golden Lock breaded shrimp, which "can be overcooked for up to ten minutes without burning," that is, darkening outside, or, even worse, "shrinking." If overcooking is not your problem, Treasure Isle has yet another breaded shrimp, Riksha, with "a holding time of over one hour." Who knows what iron-hard and impervious material that "breading" is made of. More important, who knows what's inside? Extruded shrimp has been around for years. The shrimp is ground into a paste, shaped into a large slugiform curl, and then breaded. It is only a step from extruding shrimp to extending it, and finally, to Treasure Isle reconstituted shrimp extended with FISH. The emphasis is *RB*'s own, announcing this new process by which Treasure Isle is able to "extend the shrimp naturally . . . it is said to taste like shrimp because shrimp is the primary ingredient." I have eaten extruded shrimp, and so have you if you've ever ordered a mixed-seafood platter at one of those appalling restaurants on American turnpikes—they're easy to recognize, even without the taste (which is anonymous and like leftover cream of wheat in texture), because they are such perfectly shaped little lumps and they come without tails. But, frighteningly, the picture accompanying the prose about Treasure Isle's new fabrication shows peeled shrimp, mixed red and white in color, and shaped just like fresh shrimp. Watch out for your next shrimp cocktail on the road.

Some of the ads have a greedy simplemindedness that's genuinely charming. Like this one, for French's Cattlemen's Sauce (a brownish ketchup), written, as these ads often are, in the hortatory present:

> *Chicken is what they want. With Cattlemen's it's worth more. Like 75¢ more. It couldn't be easier to fix. All you do is baste on a little Cattlemen's while you broil, bake, grill. Then call it something special like Cheyenne Chicken. It'll mean extra value to your customers. Plus an extra 75¢ margin to you!*

"When I saw how much profit my ovens were burning up," says one smiling and balding middle-aged man in a neat, twenty-year-old suit, "I had one thing to say."—MOINK. MOINK is a trade name of the Oscar Mayer Food-service Division, accompanying a trademark that looks and sounds like a pig, a turkey, and a cow all in one. And possibly tastes the same way. MOINK is precooked food. "We'll pre-fry the bacon, pre-cook those juicy smoked sausages, and even pre-slice our famous hams." The turkey breast, borne proudly by a smiling and motherly woman on a big platter, is a huge, pale, perfect mound that looks as if it has been heaped in a giant gelatin mold. And it probably has. You've eaten MOINK in lots and lots of restaurants that used to have ovens but now have higher profits.

More interesting even than MOINK are portion control and shaped meat. Colonial Beef will provide you with meat chopped and shaped into patties, breaded or unbreaded, in five different shapes: chop (which looks like a blobby pork chop), natural (which is domed on top and flat on the bottom), tapered (which looks like a large goose egg), oval (which is oval with a flat top), and hoagie (which is long and round at both ends, the better to fit on a roll). A specialty is breast of lamb, which has had a pocket cut in the thin layer of meat over the ribs of lamb, the pocket filled with ground lamb, and the bone removed. The result is something that Colonial Beef calls, complete with quotation marks, "chops." "Chops" are real meat streaked with fat on the outside, and ground lamb inside—good meat, too, insists Lou Waxman, president of Colonial Beef, in *RB:*

> When working with a shaped product it is a temptation . . . to mix in heads, cheeks, ears, weasands, spleens, glands, melts, head meat and fatty tissue. We do not do that.

The implication is that other fabricators of shaped meats, who may be supplying your local restaurant, do include all that stuff that usually goes only into pet foods. "Weasands," a word that sent me to my dictionary, turns out to be "archaic for esophagus," and "melts" is only another name for spleens—unless, and I really doubt this, Mr. Waxman means that the sperm sacs of fish are sometimes thrown into the food shaper too. It's nice to think that archaic words are being kept alive, even in one of our newest industries, and there is of course nothing wrong with any gland or weasand as food. Colonial

Beef does use meat extenders in its shaped products—soy protein, for example, and, says Mr. Waxman, "products produced do not have a 'cereal bite,' but rather a 'meat bite.'"

Mr. Waxman points out an advantage of shaped meats that some of us may have failed to recognize. There was a problem with serving veal cordon bleu in hospitals. The hospital-level recipe calls for breaded veal topped with Canadian bacon and cheese. Elderly patients had trouble chewing the Canadian bacon, said Mr. Waxman. So Colonial chopped the bacon and the cheese into the veal, breaded the patty, and now you have the same natural taste, and yet it is easy to chew. Even without teeth, like all shaped meats.

Anaprime Imitation meat is made of soy in almost any flavor you could desire: ham, chicken, beef. It will not change color, or its neat cube shape, no matter what you do to it, and it cannot shrink. No preparation. Dump it in soups, use it in salads, make it into chicken à la king. And, best of all, Anaprime has 28 percent more volume than meat. "Three quarters of a pound of Anaprime has the same plate appeal as one pound of the meat being replaced." So you have two choices—cut your portions and pocket big profits, or use the same amount of Anaprime and reap equally important benefits in "customer appreciation." Anaprime comes in large cardboard cartons that look like milk containers, so it is easy to pour, and of course it has "natural mouth feel."

Swift has a Char-proof Peperoni that puts an end to charred or curled-up edges. "The confidential spice ingredient enables it to keep its color, shape and great taste . . . up to 600° Fahrenheit." "Confidential spice ingredient" is my favorite euphemism for chemical preservatives. Thank You brand egg custard comes ready to use, in a ninety-six-ounce can—just spoon this bright-yellow lavalike material into a cup and serve, or shape first, and call it something like Mexican Flan, adding seventy-five cents to your margin.

If you run a Mexican restaurant you can use fresh avocados. You have to throw out skins and seeds, you have to hire someone to separate and mash the fruit, you have to have a supplier who will guarantee ripe avocados or else ripen your own, and you have to worry about seasonal fluctuation in prices. Or . . . you can use Calavo frozen or canned avocado pulp, which has none of those food-management disadvantages—and if your customers notice the watery taste and hydrolyzed smooth texture, they'll never complain. *You* must have noticed that taste and that texture in cheap Mexican fast-food places yourself, reader. Did you ever complain?

Knorr-Swiss does a comparison ad—"The six-minute mousse vs. the thirty-five-minute mousse." With the instant powder, "you don't have to separate eggs, melt chocolate, or beat egg whites to perfection." Just add milk and serve. There is another important difference, since the list of ingredients includes "sugar, cocoa, hydrogenated coconut oil, glyceryl-lacto esters of fatty acids . . . agar . . . artificial color . . ." But no eggs and no chocolate; you're not the only one who doesn't want to be bothered with melting and whipping.

Of course, liquid margarine is served as clarified butter with whole frozen lobster heated precooked, prereddened, and heated in a microwave (you can recognize frozen lobster: the shell has an odd flexibility, and keeps bending rather than breaking clean). But it takes a certain kind of bland mendacity to advertise "fully baked frozen warm-and-serve roll that has already been prespread with margarine for that 'cooked-in-butter flavor.'"

Ranch Hand offers a Roll-O-Burger, beef chopped and extruded into a hot-dog shape, which can be served on a hot-dog bun, needs no cooking, "can be kept warm during the day on your existing hot-dog roller grill or heated for two minutes in the microwave . . . moist and meaty with a slightly charcoal-broiled flavor." Probably extruded charcoal, chopped right into the meat.

Even real items offer opportunities for customer deception. Rich's "specially designed tins give Rich's Pies more pieshell depth and higher profiles." More impact. Less cost to you. John Morrell Food Services Quik Carv is a special ham designed so that you can slice it "as thin as you like . . . serve up mountains of customer-pleasing, smokey ham flavor without losing control of costs." And make one of those three-inch-thick sandwiches, artfully piled up with slices you can read through, which pleat down to a quarter inch under the pressure of human teeth.

Crystal Tips Ice Products advertises a large freezer with ice trays that produce "Honest Ice," a special lens-shaped ice cube, flat on one side, curved on the other, designed to minimize splashing and to "nestle in the glass for maximum displacement." In other words, it takes up more room and makes your small drinks look bigger. There are whipped-cream machines that advertise a whipped product that holds its peak for hours with or without refrigeration. And to put in it, Nestlé offers a new nondairy powder that is highly versatile. "It reconstitutes to the consistency of milk, cream or half and half."

Lest you think that all this is only an American aberration, La Prairie of France supplies thirty-one French restaurants with twenty-two IQF items that can be cooked in minutes in a microwave, eight to ten portions at a time. You have your choice of things like "curried navarin of lamb with exotic rice, duckling au cointreau with pommes croquettes, supremes of sorrel with braised hearts of lettuce, blanquette of veal 'ancient style.'" Discounts on orders of 120. And, according to the possibly Anglophobic, possibly joking writer in *QFFI,* "Delivery to London is free of charge on minimum orders of a ton."

TEN

TEST YOUR OWN

When I test a restaurant, I usually take three other people—and go to each restaurant twice. I do not think that is really necessary—restaurants charge by the meal and ought to be willing to be judged by the meal—but the more food there is on the plates, the more you have a chance to discover just where (and why) the restaurant went right (and wrong). Two people can do a good mini-review of a restaurant—though I would never write up a review on only two meals. And besides, two couples will have more fun, and more to talk about.

There are only two basic rules:

1 EVERYBODY TASTES EVERYTHING

This means you have to pass your plate of food around the table—like you do the cards when you play airplane pinochle or fish. No new person along on a test has ever looked forward to this simple little act with anything but dread. It sounds embarrassing—but it is actually, as all testers quickly find out, lots of fun. There is really something a little selfish about keeping all the food you ordered to yourself, and a little impractical too—you're always saddened that you ordered worse (if you're that kind of person) or better (if you're that other kind of person) than anyone else at the table. Passing the plates is communal and democratic and equal and sometimes hilarious—you get a little bit of lots of different things, and very frequently it is like having a very good meal, an ordinary meal and a pretty bad meal all at once. Which should surprise you the first time it happens.

There are problems—please be sure to take your knife and fork off the plate before you pass it, because otherwise they always slide and slip and once someone dropped a whole forkful of Béarnaise sauce into my wineglass where it sort of oozed up globs of fatty strings that floated to the top and the waiter, who probably had other problems besides, refused to believe it was an accident. "How could there be an accident like that?" he said. So we all felt like little kids caught playing with our food. So watch your fork, and watch your fingers—sometimes the food is cooked on the plate and the plate stays hot much longer than the food.

2 EASY ON THE BOOZE

For safety's sake, go easy on the booze—remember, you're passing food around and some of it is bound to be hot. And also do so for the test's sake. Many restaurants push booze—and make sure you wait in the bar for at least two drinks (no matter how long it takes for you to order them) before leading you to the table, where you will be asked to order another drink (by a waiter who is painfully surprised if you refuse). All those drinks are at least one and a half times as big as the drinks you make at home and made with much cheaper booze, of course. (Unless you order by brand and watch the bartender pour it, you always get the bar brand after the second drink.) By the time the food finally arrives, there is nothing you can put in your mouth that won't taste most of all like a speedrack martini.

When I test, I order a bottle of wine split among four people, and a single drink (that I leave unfinished). You know your own capacity, but if you usually have a couple of predinner drinks, you may be surprised at what you've been eating if you try your favorite restaurant sober (or soberer).

What to order is not really a problem—after all, you're doing this for yourself, so just order what you like. You'll get a better idea of the restaurant, though, if you order appetizers, entrees, desserts—and make sure that you mix them up. Some simple food so you can tell the quality of the basic ingredients, some complicated entrees to see how well the chef does with sauces, some things that make the waiter work a little so you see what the service is like.

The easiest way to demonstrate this is with a menu, and so I am going to make one up—not a real menu but the kind you can find in many many restaurants. I list real prices from 1979—they will be higher when this is published, but the relative prices are what matter:

Les Hors d'Oeuvre

Nova Scotia Smoked salmon	5.25
(sauce moutarde, served with capers and cornichons)	
Escargots Bourguignonne	4.25
Steamed mussels or clams	3.75
Fettucini Alfredo	3.50
Terrine du chef	3.75
(duck liver pâté, with ham, duck and chicken livers)	
Fruits de mer St. Jacques	4.75
(scallops, shrimp, crab and mushrooms baked in a cream sauce, lapped with cheese)	
Cherrystone clams on the half shell	3.75
Bluepoint oysters on the half shell	4.50
Shrimp cocktail	5.25

Les Potages

Soupe à l'oignon gratinée	1.50
Snapper soup	1.50
Vichyssoise	1.50

Already we know a lot about this place—it is one of those restaurants in the Northeast that started out French and slowly added some delicatessen and Italian items to the menu to keep the customers coming back.

Nova Scotia salmon is good delicatessen food and here it is priced high enough so that it should be good enough to eat. The sauce moutarde may turn out to be nothing more than a glop from a jar of Dijon, and the cornichons may be baby gherkins—but you will get a good idea of what the restaurant considers good basic ingredients. A good uncomplicated order.

Escargots—snails—are usually the highest-priced item on an expensive menu—just like shrimp cocktail is the highest priced on a cheap menu. Because women like both of them, and restaurants—sexist ever—are convinced their dates will pay extra just to make them happy. The shrimp cocktail on this menu cost more than the snails, indicating that the management knows that good shrimp cost more or that something is wrong with the snails. Snails is a possible order—semicomplicated (all you have to do is make garlic butter and not burn the snails—or their shells—in the broiler). One more plus—they're small and easy to hide if they can't be eaten.

Steamed mussels is one of the Italian specialties, and in the first place likely to be too large for an appetizer. In the second place, I never order steamed shellfish on the first visit to any restaurant—and I have never been sorry. The same goes for the oyster and clam cocktails. If everything else is fresh and good, you will want to come back anyway. And you can always have shellfish on your second trip. Remember that this stuff does not freeze well, and does not even refrigerate well—and many restaurants insist on freezing and refrigerating it. Please be warned.

Fettucini Alfredo is one of the Italian specialties and it is worth ordering to make sure you have something to eat. After all, the worst this particular dish gets is limp spaghetti in a kind of milky puddle of cottage cheese, served with a little stainless-steel bucket of powdered milk masquerading as parmesan. The price here is suspiciously low—probably means a small portion, but this is certainly a good complicated item to order. When this is good, it's excellent; and it usually is not good.

Terrine du chef is another good order—complicated enough to get the chef's whole attention, because he can simply let the waiter slice it after it is made. There are, as you can see by looking at the entree list below, lots of duck and chicken items on the menu, so there will be both duck and chicken livers to make the terrine from. The chef might keep the price low because he is proud of his work and wants everybody to try it. So it may be the best food in the house.

Fruits de mer St. Jacques sounds as if the management has discovered that the price of scallops has gone up—even of the relatively inexpensive deep-sea scallops. (Note that the menu does not say bay scallops—if it doesn't, they aren't. Frequently, when it does say bay scallops, they aren't really bay scallops either—but plain scallops are always deep-sea scallops, usually as big as golf balls, and frequently not even scallops but chunks of flesh punched out of a skate by machine.) So the management has attempted to eke things out with some baby shrimp and frozen crab. A very suspicious dish, and one that should be ordered.

The soups are easily disposed of. Never order vichyssoise the first visit—not because it will hurt you, but because there's no use paying for powdered mashed potatoes, nondairy creamer and freeze-dried chives—and that's what you get in many places. There is no beef on the menu that comes with a bone, which means that the chef would have to buy bones to make his own stock—and there is no reason to believe that any chef would do that. So if you order onion soup you are only going to get canned beef broth, which is not worth $1.50. Snapper soup is a northeastern United States specialty made from frozen turtle meat, whose purpose is to clean up all the leftover drippings and gravies from any fowl on the menu. Snappers are now an endangered species because of the popularity of this soup, which seems especially appalling because there is so little snapper meat or even snapper flavor left after all the leftovers have been thrown in the pot. In other sections of the country, this soup might be called minestrone and filled up with dried beans instead of little fibers of frozen turtle—then it is sometimes worth ordering (beans are not an endangered species) if you really like the taste of old gravy.

So, by process of elimination, we have a simplified list to choose from:

Nova Scotia salmon	simple ingredients
Escargots	semicomplicated
Fettucini Alfredo	complicated, but almost restaurant-proof
Terrine du chef	complicated
Fruits de mer St. Jacques	complicated and suspicious
Shrimp	simple ingredients

If it were my test, I would encourage people to get the salmon, the fettucini, the terrine and the fruits de mer. But almost any combination of simple and complicated dishes will give you a very good idea of what is going on in the kitchen.

Now for the entrees:

Les Entrees (of course)

Filet mignon, sauce Béarnaise	10.95
Scaloppine of veal Oscar	8.95
Poulet farci aux champignons	7.95
(whole baby chicken marinated in herbs and wine, with a light mushroom-and-cream stuffing)	
Rack of lamb (for two)	25.00
Duck à l'orange	10.50
Broiled poisson du jour, sauce amandine	8.95
Scallops Provençale	7.95
Broiled sirloin	14.50
Breast of capon maison	8.25
(stewed with mushrooms, peppers and a light tomato sauce)	
Sweetbreads financière, sauté	6.95
(with cream and truffle sauce)	
Rognons de veau, port wine sauce	5.95

This is an assembled menu—you'd rarely find the last two items on a menu that has so many Italian dishes on the rest of the list. But I put in the last two items anyway, so I can say a couple words in favor of ordering those parts of the animal's body which American cookbooks call "variety meats" and the French cookbooks call "offal"; especially in expensive French restaurants these are the best orders in the house. First of all, the chef is proud of his skill at cooking them, or he wouldn't insist that they be put on the menu. Even reading the word "sweetbread" or "kidney" is so offensive to many Americans that they grow pale or pretend to gag right at the table. Second, the chef keeps the price low (they are always the lowest prices on the menu, no matter how expensive the other ingredients) because he wants people to order it—just like his terrine. Third, the chef spends a lot of time and trouble with the sauce, more than he does on many more expensive items. And finally, if the restaurant is expensive enough, the waiter makes a lot of extra fuss about the order—because he too is happy when the chef is happy that *somebody* in America is willing to try good food. Besides all that, they are delicious.

And since you're testing this restaurant and passing the plates, you only have to eat (or turn your nose up at) one quarter of the meal—so this is a perfect time to see if you like them.

I usually try to get my guests to spread the entrees around so that we get one beef, one fowl, one fish and one veal or offal on the first visit. Sometimes looking at the menu can tell you what to leave out.

The filet, for example, is four dollars less than the sirloin. Neither says prime, so you can assume that neither is. But sirloin is a man's order traditionally—a man who is fussy about his meat. No sauce to hide the texture, and the price is high enough so that the basic ingredient ought to be (had better be) good. I usually ask the waiter the difference between the two, and usually offer to pay more if he will bring me a side of Béarnaise with my sirloin—because I want to see what the Béarnaise is like. He is usually delighted to do it, especially if someone else at the table has ordered offal.

The veal on this menu is priced much too low to bother with on a first visit. Nothing wrong with ordering suspicious food, of course, but there is likely to be enough to complain about if you order things that have a chance of being decent. Veal that costs less than the filet never does, because it can't possibly be good veal—and will wind up tasting like turkey-roll lunch meat. This particular recipe—veal Oscar—involves topping the scaloppine with cream sauce, crab and a couple stalks of asparagus. I have not been able to find out who Oscar was, but no one owes him a debt of gratitude—except the chef trying to disguise cheap meat.

The chicken is probably decent food. Chicken is almost restaurant-proof to begin with—and sitting the thing in a marinade in the refrigerator is probably the safest thing that a restaurant can do.

Rack of lamb is a clumsy item to test—two choices used up in one entree. As the price goes up, more and more places are making this a single order and bringing a little half-rack for one person. No reason why they should not have been able to do that from the beginning, of course. At this price, this should be a good order if it is available for one, at $12.50.

Duck à l'orange is a very safe dish—there's always plenty to eat. But the price is high, because this is another first date dish for women. The chicken is almost certainly a better bargain.

Always ask about the fish du jour. If it is flounder, trout or Dover sole, skip it—because those fish are the fish of *tous les jours* and are very likely to come out of a freezer. Sauce *amandine* is never anything more than slivered almonds and clarified butter at best. So this counts as a very simple dish.

Scallops Provençale is an extremely suspicious entree—first of all, how come this stuff costs $4.75 as an appetizer, even mixed up with the baby shrimp and frozen crab, and it costs only three dollars more as an entree? What is it mixed with that's cheaper? How come there's no description on the menu? The waiter will be happy to describe this thing for you, of course—but you don't need that, you only need to look down at the description of breast of capon maison to realize that the scallops Provençale is probably a heartless mess of semi-Italian stew, with the same golf-ball scallops, usually cut up in small pieces so they look like more. Scallops really can't take a lot of heavy flavors like peppers and garlic, and there is usually no such thing as a light tomato sauce in a restaurant that says it has a light tomato sauce. Skip the scallops.

But consider the breast of capon. Chicken is being used here as a substitute for the expensive veal. And really there's nothing wrong with stewing chicken with peppers and tomatoes—and nothing wrong with avoiding the pressed vealburgers that many restaurants use. Chicken is cheaper than veal, and sometimes these recipes are excellent. Even chicken breast parmesan—which sounds as ersatz as slug Bourguignonne—frequently turns out to be a big and delicious entree.

So we now have a list of possible entrees:

Poulet or breast of capon or duck	all more or less complicated
Sirloin steak with a side order of Béarnaise sauce	simple, with a complicated sauce
Fish du jour (unless it is flounder, sole or trout)	simple, with a simple sauce
one of the offal dishes	complicated

If you do not order the fish du jour, of course, you should make sure you order the fruits de mer as an appetizer—you want to have some idea of what the restaurant does to fish. And if you order the fruits de mer but the fish du jour turns out to be frozen—then change your order from the smoked Nova Scotia salmon to the shrimp cocktail. And taste the shrimp, without any cocktail sauce on it at all, before you taste the scallops. Shrimp is always frozen first if you buy it outside Texas and Louisiana, because there's a federal law against shipping fresh shrimp interstate. But some restaurants keep the shrimp around much longer than others. And disguise the taste of old shrimp by soaking them in a mix of water and lemon juice. Once you taste this without the cocktail sauce, you'll recognize it instantly—the shrimp get a sodden fibrous texture, and the taste of lemon, and another taste, as if you are having a tooth drilled at the dentist's, comes through very clearly. If the shrimp taste like that, don't eat the scallops, because they taste like that too, and you can't tell because of the sauce.

A restaurant good enough to have offal dishes would ordinarily have fresh fish that really is fresh, and I would encourage my guests to order that. If it didn't I would make sure to order the chicken and the duck both—because lots of people like duck in restaurants, and they have a right to know whether it's good or not. You won't have that problem, and the rack of lamb would be a better substitute.

Remember that you should order all the different kinds of potato that are available—sometimes baked, fried with bits of bacon or curds of cream (or more horribly, both bacon and curds), boiled, french fried, sometimes even mashed. Mashed potatoes in American restaurants are now almost always ersatz in some way, and there is no better test. French fries—simple french fries—have disappeared. What we have in their place is frozen french fries, or big chunks of potato with the skin still on the end that are deep fried but not long enough, so all they get is greasy and gray looking, and crinkle-cut french fries that seem absolutely not to be fried at all but to be simply suffering from heat exhaustion from being left in a microwave oven longer than ten seconds. Foil-wrap potatoes get a watery boiled texture to them, and it is a great deal more trouble for restaurants to make real baked potatoes, so you should look for that. Order different vegetables if there is a choice—but any restaurant that has more than two vegetables-of-the-night has nothing but canned or frozen vegetables, because the chef can't be bothered standing over ten or twelve different pots and simply drops the stuff on a steam table and lets nature and natural decomposition take its course. If the restaurant *has* more than two vegetables, order the cole slaw, the pepper hash, or the applesauce—even canned applesauce can actually be eaten.

Canned peas or, even more revolting, canned spinach, should be avoided at any cost.

Les Desserts

Cheesecake	2.00
Bloody Mary cheesecake	2.50
Strawberry cheesecake	2.25
Mousse au chocolat	2.75
Frozen Grand Marnier soufflé	3.25
Our Own Ice Cream	2.00
White-chocolate mousse	3.25
Peach Melba	2.75
Poires Hélène	2.75
Sinful chocolate lascivious decadence	3.25
From our pastry cart	3.00
Rice pudding	1.50

An impossible list, hopefully. Let's start with the worst first: flavored cheesecake. No restaurant has actually offered Bloody Mary cheesecake to my knowledge—but the profusion of cheesecakes named after cocktails is one of the most depressing developments of our time. Cheesecake straight up is a bad enough dessert, no matter how good it is. In fact, the creamier and richer, the more leaden it will lay on your stomach after a big meal, and the more you will feel that little tiny globules of cream and butter, disguised as cold sweat, are appearing on your forehead. Strawberry cheesecake is almost always horrible, but it is usually nothing more dangerous than a transparent gel with lumps of frozen red berries suspended in it that lays on the top of the regular cheesecake like a thin puddle of rubbery blood. But cheesecake flavored with alcohol—I have actually tasted Amaretto, grasshopper, godfather and Cherry Heering and I live in fear of finding dry martini cheesecake on some menu yet—cheesecake flavored with alcohol is either so loaded with alcohol that it is in the process of separating, like day-old eggnog, or it is artificially flavored, or hideously artificially colored, or all three. Chocolate cheesecake, not listed on this menu, is fading from many other menus, too—possibly because it tastes like sour, spoiled chocolate pudding. Chocolate mousse is a good test; it should have a texture of melted chocolate and beaten egg whites mixed together, and it should not taste like Jell-O Instant Chocolate Pudding, though many do. Frozen Grand Marnier soufflé is a much better idea than cheesecake if you want a boozy dessert, and frozen soufflés are so easy to make and keep that it is almost always among the best desserts on the list of a mediocre restaurant. Homemade ice cream and ices are also a very good idea—order the weirdest-sounding flavor, it's usually the dessert chef's special idea and you usually get an extra-big serving. White-chocolate mousse was a menu fad in New York City early in the eighties. Mimi Sheraton, restaurant critic for the New York *Times,* complained bitterly that it looked like raw beef fat—which is true. But if you like a very sweet and very mild chocolate taste, it was kind of fun, and like most fad desserts usually came with some extra inducement, like crispy little cookies or a drool of raspberry syrup. Peach Melba is one of the worst desserts in any restaurant. The peach is almost always canned, the ice cream is always second rate, and the raspberry syrup tastes like a melted cents-off sale-brand of supermarket jelly. It is disappearing. Poires Hélène (sometimes Poir Helene and on one menu actually listed as Poivre Helen) is disappearing too, but it is not nearly as bad. Ask if the pear is fresh—canned pears are almost as bad as canned peaches—and give it a try. Sinful chocolate lascivious decadence is likely to be one of those restaurant double-chocolate cakes that seem to be trying to become fudge without knowing how; usually it turns out to be little more than an extra-rich chocolate brownie with a thick chocolate sauce. And it is usually very good. But people who call this food sinful or use sexual terms to describe it know something more or something less about sex than I do. Some food tastes wonderful, I admit, but surely that's not *all* there is to decadence and sin. Still, this is a good dessert usually, and a good test. If there is something in a brioche or in puff pastry among the appetizers, and the pastry was good, the dessert pastries are likely to be superb. Be sensible about fruit tarts, though; if you order raspberry in the dead of winter, you're getting raspberry jam. Apple is often the best in winter, because apples store well. Kiwi, another fad foodstuff, seems to me to be a fruit that is never ripe and always expensive; so if you order a kiwi tart you get less and worse fruit than in any other. Rice pudding, the last on this list, is almost never the least. It really is a way of getting rid of leftovers. I have never seen an instant or premixed rice pudding, and never expect to see one; this stuff is too cheap as it is. So the chef usually tries to make it as attractive and appetizing as possible; and even in a bad restaurant, rice pudding is restaurant-proof: even *bad* rice pudding is pretty good stuff.

A word about whipped cream: whipped cream is cream that has been whipped until stiff. Many Americans have apparently never tasted the stuff, because when I say that the whipped cream is not natural in a restaurant I sometimes get a letter from a customer saying it is so natural; and more often one from the restaurant owner, too, offering to prove that the whipped cream is natural—by showing me it says so, right on the can. Canned whipped cream doesn't taste like whipped cream. You can try this yourself by buying heavy cream, whipping it and comparing it to the canned cream that you buy in the supermarket. One tastes like whipped cream; one doesn't. Do not buy whipping cream if you want to know what whipped cream tastes like, of course. This is America, and whipping cream—which is bought by many restaurants—has been loaded with chemicals to make it stand up longer and peak better. And to make it taste less like whipped cream. Some restaurants hold real whipped cream by whipping in sugar, some by whipping in arrowroot. They both taste better than the chemicals used in whipping cream. And to me, they both taste worse than plain whipped cream.